Transformational CPR

Transformational CPR

A Guide To Awaken The Heart

Maya Rasak, MFT

The information contained in this book is intended to be educational and not for diagnosis, prescription, or treatment of any health disorder whatsoever. This information should not replace consultation with a competent healthcare professional.

Transformational CPR may be purchased for educational, business or sales promotional use. For information, please contact us at: maya@soulintegration.biz

ISBN-13: 978-1481079075

ISBN-10: 1481079077

First Edition

10 9 8 7 6 5 4 3 2 1

Dedicated to Mommy dearest,
who gifted me life not once,
but twice.

CONTENTS

PART ONE

The First Step in CPR
(Consciousness—Checking for a Pulse)

PART TWO

The Second Step in CPR
(Presence—Mouth-to-Mouth:
Trying to Survive Through Relationships)

PART THREE

The Third Step in CPR
(Receptivity—Awakening the Heart to Receive More Love)

CONCLUDING THOUGHTS

Acknowledgments

Without my dear mother, this book would not have been possible. She gave me not only life, but also unconditional love in times when I could not find love within. She has been the backbone and strength in our family through dark and light, but always holding the torch silently for us to find our way.

My deepest gratitude to the many teachers I have had throughout my life in Advaita Vedanta, Mahayana Buddhism, Yoga Sutras of Patanjali, Hatha Yoga, meditation, psychology, and many other practices I have been fortunate enough to inhale. Without these ancient practices, I would not be the person I am today, nor would I have been able to guide others on their path.

A special thanks to Jack Rosenberg, Beverly Morse, and The Institute of Integrative Body Psychotherapy, where I have grown and learned so much about myself but mostly how to breathe deeply.

Thank you to Korena Ellis, who, with much love, designed the image for the book cover. She contributed to the manuscript by reading early drafts and keeping me focused. Her love and support were an asset to my creative process.

Lauran Hoffman, writer and filmmaker, assisted me in a grueling final cut before handing it off to the editor. She gave me numerous helpful notes about trimming out the excess, teaching me the value in "economy of speech", according to E.B. White. I am grateful to her for the time and energy she put in on the final stages in making this book a reality.

Yumana Yunes, who has been an angel by spending countless hours perfecting the cover and the interior of the book until I was finally won over. Her patience and support was a total asset to the book.

Bryony Shaw, writer and therapist, read my first draft and gave me honest and helpful feedback. Her encouragement throughout my life has been a huge inspiration.

Thank you to my big sis Janet, who has always been someone I've looked up to. She has been an advocate of all my crazy endeavors.

Thanks to Writing Coach Rachel Reznick and Writers

on Fire for intelligent and insightful feedback on various chapters throughout the book's early stages.

I'm grateful to Ann Rodgers, my friend, for introducing me to God and the world of meditation many years ago. It was her guidance, patience, and love that championed my spiritual growth beyond all measure.

Lastly, I am eternally grateful for my constant connection to the almighty spirit for guiding me each and every day of my life and keeping me on purpose.

Introduction

There are many types of psychotherapy. Most people aren't aware of the variety of modalities when shopping for a therapist. There are cognitive-behavioral, object-relations, intersubjectivity, psychoanalysis, narrative, and so on. In spite of these numerous modalities, most therapists use only conversation and don't engage the body or the soul. I believe we are holistic beings and need to be treated in that manner. When working with people, I think it is essential to examine the whole being: body, mind, and spirit. We are spiritual beings living a human experience within molecular bodies.

We are living in a world of form and material priorities; however, it's important to maintain a connection to our authentic self. What is at the center of every one of us? Our core, authentic self is our center and a place of peace and well-being. Anything other than that state emanates from distracting thoughts or false beliefs conjured up in the mind. Our detachment from our authenticity can only exist from a belief that we are separate from it. When we are caught up in memories or worrying about the future, we're not present. This moment is the only thing that is real. The past and the future have no relevance to the present moment. When we are present, we eradicate our suffering and align our thoughts with perfect peace and joy at the center of our being.

Knowledge of our past may assist us in avoiding making similar mistakes in the present or in the future. Insight into our own psyche can be very useful and help us change our behavior, however the type of therapy I provide is quite unique. It combines psychological insight with somatic work, yoga philosophy, and existential elements.

From this combination, a system developed that I refer to as Transformational CPR. This system was born out of my individual therapy as well as my experience as a clinician. Many years of yoga training, Eastern spiritual practices, such as Mahayana Buddhism and Advaita Vedanta, as well as a certification in Integrative Body Psychotherapy have all contributed to the work I do today.

Transformational CPR is a metaphor for a process that brings us back to a state of being, which most people are still seeking, though they already have it at their core. My passion is dedicated to awakening individuals to a more conscious state. In the same way we can revive and awaken the unconscious body with cardiopulmonary resuscitation (CPR), we can activate the spiritual heart, thus gaining access to everlasting peace and joy.

The "C" in CPR stands for "consciousness." By allowing one's awareness to surface, one can dramatically improve patterns of unconscious behavior. An unconscious pattern may be derived from a thought or belief. Judgments, wishful thinking, and self-defining narratives can create dissonance and resistance, placing our consciousness in a "suffering mind." Expanding and strengthening our consciousness not only sheds light on who we truly are but is also instrumental in rooting us in the present.

I've deemed the "P" in CPR to represent the concept of "presence." When we are not present, energy cannot flow freely in the body, thus creating lethargy. With stagnation, comes psychological blocks and dis-ease. Dis-ease is experienced as a discomfort in the body and an agitation in the mind. With prolonged dis-ease comes disease and sickness. A negative pattern can ensue, distracting us from being fully present. It's common to regurgitate the past and feel remorse, resentment, or guilt about past events. Its also natural to project into the future, feeling anxious and fearful about something we imagine may happen. Guilt and regret are feelings linked to the past, while worry, doubt, and fear are feelings of the future, but remember that the past and future have limited relevance in the present. These feelings only have power over us when we allow our minds to wander backward and forward. There are many skills I teach to ground people in the present moment. Some techniques include deep breathing and movement, which help to define where the blocks and holding patterns reside in the body, so they can be discharged and the pattern reorganized in a healthy way.

The "R" in CPR stands for "receptivity". Once present, we are without negative or colored filters, enabling us to receive life in its pure form, much like a child, who experiences everything fresh, free from preconceived ideas. This enables us to align with opportunities that may otherwise be missed. Instead of blocking or resisting, we become a vessel for limitless creativity and unconditional love, and our hearts open, providing an environment to give and receive love more freely, thus gaining access to deeper intimacy. We feel more integrated because it is here that we connect to our authentic core self. While connected, we have access to the spiritual and emotional nourishment we all crave.

The function of Transformational CPR is to reawaken the emotional heart and create wholeness and integration where there was once fragmentation and separation. It provides people with the necessary tools for achieving and maintaining a state of well-being. Very few people, if any, had all of their needs met in childhood. This lack prompts us to seek fulfillment from outside sources rather than turn within where true contentment resides. This work is designed for those who desire more joy and fulfillment and for those who truly want to manifest their dreams. Transformational CPR will empower you to reclaim what is your birthright.

Preface
Sweating Prayers

Our task is not to seek for love,
but merely to seek and find all
the barriers within yourself that you
have built against it.
~ Rumi

It was an auspicious day in the middle of nowhere. Mystic, an intense and determined medicine woman led us through a sacred journey. Our close-knit group had traveled from Los Angeles to Taos, New Mexico, to witness our friends' walk down the aisle to start married life together. Mystic didn't smile the entire afternoon. She was focused on every aspect of the ceremonial sweat lodge, making sure no one left without a full experience. Her eyes were liquid-nitrogen blue and vividly contrasted her long white hair. Some of the crevices in her face were as deep as the gorge we had recently hiked. Her skin revealed obvious exposure to the harshest elements in nature.

The handpicked selection of rocks had been smoldering

in the fire all day and was scalding by the time we arrived. The fire-keeper had difficulty keeping the fire contained in the high winds but was dedicated to heating the precious stones. Our group was late in arriving, and in the interest of time, we were thrown in without preparation. The man-made dome we entered was constructed of pliable willow branches. A variety of animal skins had been placed over the dome-like structure so perfectly that not an ounce of air could escape.

Nothing brings up my claustrophobia quite the way a sweat lodge does. I assumed there would be four rotations, as usual. The one relieving thought was knowing that after each cycle, the flap on the door would be opened, in order to allow the cool air from outside to enter before the next round of sweat-filled prayers. There were too many people in an enclosed space, and the heat intensified as the smoldering rocks were brought in, one by one, at the start of each round. As soon as I antici-pated the flap on the door closing, I began choking on my fear. My blood-engorged head and soaking palms indicated there would be no turning back. It was proof I was committed. The ball rolling around in my stomach was gaining momentum. My heart was thumping so loudly I feared it might distract Mystic, who was directly opposite me. There was nowhere to hide, no way to divert my attention. I was forced to confront myself.

Once the door was closed, Mystic poured water on the hot rocks, creating a bed of steam and heat. The number of rocks brought into the center pit at the start of each round was increased incrementally, providing a gradation of intensity. The challenge to stay present grew exponentially as my mind wrestled to slip off to a faraway place. Beaten, I joined in the singing and chanting. I didn't know what I was saying, but the chanting helped me stay in my body, preventing my mind from escaping.

During round three, Mystic revealed a poignant story. Inhaling the scent of cedar and sage, I absorbed her tale with all five senses on high alert, each pore in my body wide open. I was in a completely receptive state to hear Mystic's story.

***

When God had finished creating the universe, which consisted of plants and animals, he contemplated his next step. While creating man, he realized there was a gift he wanted to give them, but he wasn't sure whether human beings were ready. He decided to hide the precious cargo where he knew no one would think to look until it was time. He pondered the best hiding place imaginable. He offered the question out loud to all earthly creatures.

A giant whale emerged from the ocean floor, boasting, "I have the best solution. I will hide it in the depths of the ocean where humans definitely won't find it." God said, "No, man will be deep-sea diving soon. That won't work."

A bald eagle swooped down from the heavens and said, "I will fly it all the way to the moon where they will never be able to go." God thought for a moment and said, "No, that won't work either. Man will develop aircraft and the space shuttle and will visit the moon someday."

Finally, a tiny beaver shuffled over and squealed, "I know a perfect place that humans would never think to look." All three of them turned and inquired, "Where? Where is this hiding place?" The beaver replied smugly, "Place the gift in here," and he pointed to his heart. "They will never think to look inside themselves."

***

I remained motionless; sweat covering my skin, tears rolling down my cheeks, awed by the simplicity and the gravity of this tale. Reflecting over the course of my life, I was saddened by having lost sight of the gift in side so long ago. More important, I was struck by the recent discovery of my authentic self and learning to rely on its presence even in some of my darkest hours.

We all start out completely connected to love. As babies, that's all we know. We're literally bundles of love. At what point do we separate from that gift? How is it that years later, we are all still desperately seeking that which we already have?

I spent years looking for love in all the wrong places, just like the song says. I looked to my relationships. I tried achieving fame and fortune. I thought greater success, more money, and validation from the outside would bring me love. But each path led to a dead end. Each dead end perpetuated my endless search and brought about my ultimate disillusionment.

Writing this book has deepened my understanding of what causes people to lose faith in the connection to something so vital to their existence. It's allowed me to demystify the treasure inside of me and to finally "call off the search," as one of my mentors advised me. In doing so, I continue to diminish suffering in my life, and I assist others in finding their truth so they can light their own way.

This book is a roadmap to lasting fulfillment. While on the path, it's important to recognize all the things that distract us, pulling us off purpose. Though freedom is our natural state, the beliefs and coping skills that have become habituated over time can quickly derail us into a state of fragmentation, causing us to stray from the fully integrated authentic self at the core of our being. Once we feel separate, it's difficult to regain faith that total peace lays at the center of our consciousness.

This book lays out a step-by-step process that teaches us not only how to recognize when we are off center but, more important, how to get ourselves plugged back in so we can experience deep inner peace and a feeling of connection at all times. The truth requires diligence, courage, and constant awareness. We are taught to believe that happiness and love come from outside soures, but once we experience the treasure inside, at the heart center, it's difficult to return to a state of ignorance.

It's exhausting participating in the illusion that we are separate from love, and yet we continue to play that game repeatedly. All of my injuries from childhood and my desperate attempts at working them out through my relationships catalyzed my ability to stop searching and abide in my inner stillness. I realized the love that existed in my core and the only way to access it was to stop chasing anything outside and become still. It's my responsibility to continue chipping away all the layers that keep me from that eternal source of love. Realization alone is not ultimately satisfying, but it gives me faith when I feel a separation and crave "anything" to fill the void. My big realization was awakening to the undamaged part inside, the discovery that love exists as me, eternally present.

It was CPR that revived my heart, restoring me to consciousness when I almost drowned as a young girl, but it was Transformational CPR that activated my emotional heart, restoring my faith in eternal, everlasting love.

PART ONE

*The First Step in CPR—Consciousness
(Checking for a Pulse)*

Chapter 1
Mommy and Me

My mother had been cooking for days. She was throwing a dinner party that evening. My father's cousin was in the country, and Mom wanted to create a special evening. The dining-room table had been set for two days with our finest china. She even pulled out the sterling silverware. My mother, Mary, was born on Christmas Day. This should give you a clue about who my mother is. She was always organized and prepared for everything well in advance, twenty minutes early to every event, always doing the right thing, wanting to make sure everyone was happy. It drove my father crazy, but also was what he loved most about her. Mom was preparing the last-minute touches for the guests who would soon arrive to fill our dining room with wine-induced laughter and long-winded conversations about the Old Country.

The guests of honor were my dad's first cousin, Hannah, and his wife, Ida. They were visiting from Beirut, Lebanon. Ida's most defining feature was the large gap between her two front teeth, which was visible when she smiled or laughed, as she often did. She was a chain smoker, finishing one cigarette with her yellowing fingernails and lighting up the next with the butt of the previous one. This explained the throaty rasp in her laugh. Ida drank heavy Turkish coffee, the kind that would keep a spoon standing well past dessert.

Hannah had his set of habits, most notably keeping his left hand hidden in his front pants pocket, jiggling obscure objects. One day, I finally got the courage to ask him what was in his pocket, and he pulled out a strand of beads made of pure ebony.

In times of stress, when American men reach for Valium, Arab men are likely to reach into their pocket for a string of worry beads. The Masbaha consists of either thirty-three or ninety-nine beads, unlike the 108 that's so common to the mala beads of the Buddhists. Worry beads have enough slack in the string so that as each bead is released by the index finger and thumb, it taps its neighbor with an emphatic click. The snaps themselves lack character, but their cadence and periodic pauses express a range of emotions: agitated nervousness, thoughtful meditation, placid boredom, mounting impatience, burning hostility, and a myriad of expressions in between. The Arab's Masbaha is a natural extension of his personality and a tangible means of getting his point across without actually saying anything. Many Middle Eastern men feel undressed without a set of their own.

Hannah explained to me that the thirty-three-bead Masbaha represents the thirty-three years of Christ's earthly existence, while those of ninety-nine beads, like his, represent the thirty-three years multiplied by the three manifestations of God the Father, God the Son, and the Holy Ghost.

Also joining us for dinner that evening, were my uncle John, (the family doctor), my aunt Gloria, and my cousin Jon. Like us, they were Lebanese Americans. Aunt Glow always seemed to exhaust everybody with her chatter and incessant gossip. It drove my mother insane, but she always managed a polite smile. She could only handle Glow in small doses. They lived a block from us, so this presented a challenge. I was looking forward to seeing my cousin Jon. He and I would make up musical skits and perform them for our families. I couldn't wait to show him the new game that my brother Rick and I had invented.

None of the children, such as myself, Jon, Hannah's kids, and my brother Rick, would be invited to sit at the dining-room table with the adults. We were placed at the kitchen table instead and ate off the everyday plates with the common cutlery. The intoxicating smell of Arabic food permeated our entire house. It was a combination of pine nuts toasting, onions sautéing in a skillet with brown butter, and a lamb roasting in the oven.

Our five-bedroom Beverly Hills home in Trousdale Estates sat on an acre of land all surrounding a rather large centerpiece, the swimming pool. Our house was L-shaped, and the pool could be seen from practically every room, allowing easy access to the backyard. My brother Rick and I were playing in the yard on what seemed like a perfect afternoon. I was only three years old. Rick was four years my senior, but I worshiped him and followed him the way a shadow tracks its owner. When he started school, I begged my mother to let me go with him because I couldn't stand to be apart from him. He was my playmate, my best friend, my confidant, and my protector.

Rick and I were playing catch the monkey, our new ball game, and he decided it would be funny to push me into the swimming pool as I caught the monkey. The fact that I hadn't yet learned to swim didn't make it as amusing to my mother.

My mother, impeccably dressed, made up like a Hollywood starlet, donning a flowing gown and heels, sensed danger afoot. The noise sealed her course of action, forcing her to bolt full gallop to the pool's edge.

It didn't take long before I ran out of breath. I was struggling to make my way to the surface, but all the flailing I was doing didn't impact my rapid sinking to the bottom of the pool. Terrified, I gasped for air. I could hear the faint laughter of my brother from above me, and the splash from my mother, who, without hesitation, jumped into the deep end. Things faded quickly, until I felt a sweet surrender. Everything became still. My mother, with flattened hair and a makeup-streaked face grabbed my limp body and yanked me from the water.

She looked at my lifeless body and instantly sprang into action. CPR was designed to sustain breathing and pulse in a victim of cardiac arrest, suffocation, drug overdose, poisoning, choking, or, as in my case, drowning.

Any trained individual can administer the procedure. A continuous flow of oxygenated blood is required for normal functioning of the brain. Lack of oxygen supply for four minutes impedes brain functioning, which entirely ceases at seven minutes. CPR helps provide a regular flow of oxygen to the brain and heart.

Fortunately, Mom had taken a CPR course many years before, though she had never actually put it to use on a live body, let alone her daughter's. That was about to change.

After making sure I was completely unconscious (the first step in CPR), she opened the passageway to my lungs by pulling my head back and began to breathe life back into me. Breath by breath, into my mouth she blew, trying to get me present (the second step in CPR), but there was still no sign of life. By this point, my mother was so frantic if I could have come back to life to calm her down, I would have. This dynamic was representative of our relationship. I was always making sure she was okay, never wanting to tax her already over-burdened life as a mother of six. I quickly learned to abandon my needs to avoid adding more stress to her life.

In the third and final step, she pumped my chest with her hands, one planted on top of the other, in the hopes of reactivating my heart. She was trying desperately to bring me back to a state of conscious-ness by alternating chest compressions with mouth-to-mouth breathing. Crying hysterically, she prayed that her CPR skills would be sufficient. After several attempts to activate my heart and get things circulating, I took my first gasp of air. Coughing, I bolted upright, spitting out the water that had seeped into my lungs.

While I was sinking to the bottom of the pool, I had a flash that I would never see my mama again. With that thought came a gripping sensation all the way from my bowels up to my throat. I was a tangled web of nerves, frayed at all ends. But there she was, hanging over my trembling body with a look of concern. What a relief to open my eyes and see her tear-stained cheeks as she smiled at me. Everything was going to be okay because there was my mom and she would always protect me.

I was back, fully awake. Colors were brighter, and objects appeared in sharp focus. The memory of what had happened came flooding back in an instant—the image of my brother shoving me off the edge of the pool, the sound of his cruel laughter once I hit the water, my mom jumping in and her gown blowing up underwater, all of it. But one disturbing thought continued to plague me. My hero brother, the one I adored beyond all measure, had betrayed me and broken our sacred bond of trust. Why he would want to hurt me was beyond my comprehension. Perhaps, it was his anger at being eclipsed the day I was born. The disappointment seeped into every cell of my body where it would remain for many years to come. Trauma can happen at any time, and it will lie dormant in the body as we age until something triggers it. The knot forming in my belly was preventing me from crying, but I ached in a way I didn't understand.

Dinner was a blur that evening. I can't remember much except that the dinner party went on as if nothing had happened. All I knew was that I was back, but something had changed forever. I had my first recognition that life was not completely safe. My mother could not always protect me, hard as she tried. I held my breath and tightened every muscle in my body to avoid the unbearable feelings that accompanied that thought.

That coping strategy got me through my childhood. Unfortunately, I became so adept at it as an adult that I cut myself off from my authentic self. I realized I couldn't trust the world the way I once had. My innocence had been robbed the moment I hit the water. I spent the next thirty years trying to get my innocence back.

Chapter 2
Coping Strategies

Throughout childhood, most of us develop coping skills in order to deal with difficult situations. These defenses helped us survive our childhood, but in adulthood, those trusty strategies, which seemed to protect us from enemy forces, actually become barriers to obtaining our true desires.

No matter how aware our parents were, few people, if any, had all their needs met in childhood. The behaviors that protected us when we were young have become so ingrained by adulthood that the instant we're triggered by something unpleasant that reminds us of child-hood, we react automatically, blinding ourselves from experiencing things in their pure form. Our perception taints the way we see everything, and without awareness, it's common to interpret things based on our history. When we are able to experience things in the present moment, the Zen masters refer to that state as "beginner's mind." Beginner's mind keeps us humble but learning. When we fail to recognize that our world is colored by our prior experience, we remain helpless victims of circumstance.

As early as a few months old, babies begin developing their first beliefs, behaviors, feelings, and even body responses, which will become rigid patterns over time. In adulthood, we tend to reenact the coping skills we learned in childhood, but without healthy role models, handling difficult emotions can be precarious. Many of the strategies we learned were maladaptive and not rela-tional, making life and our intimate relationships more challenging.

Babies who appear to be spacing out might be exemplifying a child's feeble attempt to deal with overwhelming feelings and parents who were unresponsive to those feelings. Spacing out is one of the only defenses available to the infant. It's clearly a preverbal mechanism since language isn't accessible at this stage of development. This strategy becomes the preferred habit in dealing with uncomfortable feelings in the future, simply because it was ingrained early on. Those children, once they've become adults, have learned to space out or temporarily leave their bodies when they feel rejected or abandoned. They will do anything but remain present in order to avoid experiencing the painful feelings that often accompany perceived rejection.

Children are unequipped to handle most of their thoughts and feelings unless they had parents who could accurately mirror those feelings without trying to fix or change them. Children need to feel safe expressing their feelings. When they get punished, shamed, or criticized for expressing their emotions, children falter in their ability to cope. They learn to ignore their feelings, relegating them to the "you are not important file." This instigates faulty thinking (the feeling of being unimportant) and yet becomes the child's reality as he or she grows up. Unfortunately, children always blame themselves, believing they are defective somehow. They feel separate from the peaceful, loving truth of their authentic self since they have spent so much time in a split-off state. Later on in life, they spend years trying to remove the excess baggage they've acquired in order simply to connect to the essential self again.

An old colleague of mine, Kevin's, is a great example. He was born during the Dr. Spock era when parents learned to put their child to bed after a feeding and diaper change. Parents were instructed not to disturb their children for three hours, even if they cried. Kevin's parents tried their best to follow Dr. Spock's advice on child rearing as closely as possible. Parents of this generation were advised to feed and change diapers every three hours but were in no way to interrupt the three-hour window.

Kevin was put in his crib one evening after being fed and having his diaper changed. He went to sleep feeling content. Approximately an hour later, he woke up from a nightmare. Startled, he began to scream and cry. Mom was on the other side of the door listening but knew she had two hours before she should disturb her child. In keeping with Dr. Spock's rules, she waited while Kevin grew more agitated.

What happens to the infant at this point? He wonders, what is wrong with me? Why aren't my parents coming to rescue me? Don't I matter? Am I that ineffectual? He develops his first belief early on. Following that thought, he develops a behavior. After crying for a long while with no one responding, over time, he learns to give up. Naturally, from these negative thoughts, certain feelings will be provoked. He feels angry, sad, and enraged. Lastly, what happens in the boy's body while these thoughts and feelings stir is a tightening of all the muscles to prevent him from feeling his discomfort. His diaphragm shuts down, and as a result, his breathing becomes shallow. Over time, this whole pattern becomes concretized. Patterns get organized in a certain way because of circumstances and our reactions to those events. The body has cellular memory. Through repetition, our patterns become entrenched, resulting in automatic responses to the same or similar occurrences.

As an adult, whenever Kevin feels abandoned in some way by someone, he shuts down and withdraws. Any perceived rejection on his part would naturally set off this learned pattern from childhood. He ignores the feelings of not being important because they are intolerable. Instead, Kevin tenses up and his breathing becomes shallow. When his girlfriend denies him a date, he is instantly triggered. This rejection reminds him of his early days with his mother. Regardless of his girlfriend's reasoning, he feels abandoned and his childhood wound is reopened. He is no longer present but fragmented, back in the past, retraumatized by the current event. He overreacts because he's dragging his past injuries into the present, responding as though it were a crisis.

Someone else who didn't have high abandonment might feel disappointment, but being turned down for a date wouldn't feel like the end of the world; it wouldn't instigate a termination of the relationship. On a scale of one to ten, if Kevin's issues of abandonment are already at a level eight, resulting from his past experiences, then all someone needs to do is something as low as a level two in order for him to perceive it as a crisis. What should be a two now becomes a ten. This is an example of how our perceptions insidiously cloud our experiences. It's difficult to assimilate information in a neutral manner without coloring our canvas with preconceived ideas.

If we are able to identify our triggers and coping skills, instead of habitually reacting negatively, we can respond with the recognition that our past wounds are in the past and need not fragment us presently.

Chapter 3
Innocence

Starting back as early as age five, I remember "the birthday" that broke my heart and made the remaining birthdays to come events I would soon dread. We all have things from childhood that scarred us for the future, even the simplest thing that has a resounding echo and causes our hearts to harden.

The house was empty, except for Mom and me; we were in the kitchen, baking my birthday cake. In reality, she was mixing and baking, while I was licking the bowl clean of (my favorite) chocolate frosting. I can remember being slowly hypnotized by the swirling electric beater rotating and whipping the chocolate into a frenzied mound. Mom had just hung up the phone with my father, who assured her he would be home by 6:00 p.m., extra early, to celebrate my birthday since the rest of the family was away.

My mom had prepared a dinner consisting of all my favorite foods. Warming in the oven was elbow macaroni dripping with gooey, velvety cheese. A golden-brown chicken lay roasting in it's own juices, flanked with rosemary sprigs and baby apricots. The fruit melted across the animal carcass perfectly, creating the most amazing sticky, tart, and gooey mess. My mom's infamous mixed green salad always included a variety of fresh herbs handpicked from our garden. She made sure there was always a salad, drenched in fresh lemon juice, cold pressed virgin olive oil, fresh cracked pepper, and Celtic sea salt. She asked me to toss the salad, which I happily did because it always guaranteed I could taste as I tossed.

Now that we were done preparing the food and everything was in the oven baking or warming, "we can relax," my mother said. We waltzed into the den to watch the local news while we waited for my father's return home. My mom enjoyed sipping her glass of Chardonnay, which she always had at this time of day with her one cigarette. She said this was her time to enjoy herself after her work was done and before my father returned home. All I could think about were the fumes of chocolate cake filling my nostrils and what my dad was going to get me for my fifth birthday. Before long, the telephone rang. It was my father calling to inform us that he was going to be late.

I couldn't mask my disappointment. My mother attempted to comfort me with her usual cheery optimism, telling me how we had to make the best of things no matter how difficult it might seem. I knew she was right, but it only infuriated me. "We can't change the circumstance, so we might as well just accept it and not let it ruin the day, honey." Although her words were meaningless at the time, they would become one of my most used mantras twenty-five years later.

An hour later and another hunger notch on her belt, my mother's patience was worn thin, and she decided to have my father paged at the country club, inquiring about his tardiness. While playing cards with the boys, he screamed, "Damn it, Mary, I'm losing, and I'm just trying to get ahead to bring home something nice for my baby girl."

I knew that my father wasn't coming home to celebrate my birthday. I was like a soufflé that couldn't rise to the occasion, saggy and deflated. This was the moment when I began telling myself that I was unimportant. "If he really loved me, he would be home to celebrate my birthday." My mother and I ate dinner without him. I managed a conversation, in spite of the vise-grip on my throat. The slightest sound caused me to cock my head in the direction of the front door; I was anticipating my dad would walk through it at any moment. I knew he wouldn't, but I never stopped hoping.

I couldn't get any consolation from my mother. We finished dinner without my father. Ignoring my long face, Mom lit the candles on my birthday cake and sang her solo with a big smile plastered across her face. I learned well how to ignore my disappointment, but inside, my guts were churning. Pretending like everything was all right, I blew out the candles on my homemade birthday cake. Using my parents as role models, I learned early on to negate my feelings. I learned to abandon myself. Not only did my dad miss dinner, but Mom alone put me to bed and kissed me good night. My birthday was over!

I was off somewhere in dreamland when my father finally made it home. God knows what time it was when he entered my room to wake me. Still drowsy, I opened my eyes to see my father grinning at me. In his hand, he held a crisp one-hundred-dollar bill, which he couldn't wait to place into my five-year-old palm. This was my consolation prize. At that time, my father's fortune had been swept away in the stock market and he was struggling to keep our home and lifestyle. He gave me a big hug and with that a "Happy birthday, sweetheart." I didn't quite know what to say except for, "Thanks, Dad." I tried my best to appear excited, slipping on my "happy mask" to hide my despair. After all, Daddy looked so elated about his winnings and the ability to hand it over to his little girl.

The realization that love can come and go so easily terrified me. My well-being was reliant upon other people's actions, which felt unsafe because other people were unreliable, even those I cared about. I wasn't able to control their behavior. The dissapointments caused me to shut my heart down bit by bit. I grew accustomed to ignoring my feelings. I learned to abandon myself in much the same way that my caregivers ignored my feelings when I was a child. It was not that they weren't good parents—they showed up and provided for me—but I got the message that it was not safe to express myself authentically. As a child, I didn't learn how to tolerate painful emotions. I observed the adults around me in denial of their feelings, unable to tolerate emotions, and therefore learned how to hide my own. I learned so well that I lost touch with myself. I lost sight of the gift within, and I perfected the art of self-betrayal.

Chapter 4
The Art of Self-Betrayal

Self-betrayal can be compared to a loss of consciousness because when we self-abandon, we go unconscious; we tune out. It's as if there's no pulse in the body. No one is taking care of the injured child within us, and that can be terrifying. Checking out, instead of acknowledging our feelings, is an automatic reaction that most of us have become adept at, unless we had strong role models who learned how to cope with discomfort. If our parents couldn't recognize, acknowledge, and mirror back our feelings when we were scared, sad, or lonely, we didn't learn the skills necessary to take care of ourselves emotionally. When the little child inside of us gets angry, becomes afraid, or feels alone, we ignore him. We choose not to notice, hoping it will dissipate if we don't pay any attention. It's learned behavior. We don't allow that child to express his feelings, and we don't let him know that we will take care of him. We ignore our inner child in much the same way our parents disregarded our feelings when we were children. It's human behavior to repeat what we know.

Disconnecting is problematic because we lose access to the sense of well-being at our core, which is what makes the body feel alive and animated. We leave the scared child alone to cope in a chaotic world, which results in a deadening in the body. We cut off our life force. We stop breathing and armor up, creating tension in the body, while shutting down our air supply. The scared child inside feels unattended to, which naturally leaves us feeling anxious. Upon injury, most of us decide to evacuate rather than experience the uncomfortable feelings that arise.

Worse still, we miss the opportunity for true healing if we blame others for our feelings, holding them accountable for how badly we feel. We hand our power over to our "perpetrator" and complain about our self-inflicted victimhood. Holding expectations or negative judgments about other people gives us all the justification we need to continue harboring resentments toward them. As long as we adhere to these ideas of blame, any possibility of rectifying our situation remains elusive.

Whether cut off from our emotions or holding a grudge toward another person, we remain stuck, negating the present moment. Resistance to our emotions shows up in many ways. Thoughts are a common way that we distract ourselves from our feelings. If we were capable of experiencing the feelings that arise without judgments and mental interpretations, we could remain present and integrated. We would be able to take care of the child inside by acknowledging his feelings, not deeming those feelings "bad or wrong." Without trying to change our feelings, we could nurture the inner child who didn't get validation from his parents. Taking responsibility for our feelings gives us the opportunity to change our situation without waiting for someone else to change. We don't have to become hostage to someone else's harsh actions or unkind words. We can become hosts to the loving perfection within, which, in turn, determines how we feel in any given situation.

Being connected to the infinite source is the only thing that brings us peace. Otherwise, we allow the world of the finite to continue deluding us, creating our unhappiness. Everything in life is temporary, including feelings. If we don't add our opinions or narratives, feelings arise and just as quickly dissipate back to where they came from. This action of surrendering to what is present, instead of resisting, prevents us from fragmenting and allows us to stay in integrity with the truth, thereby reducing anxiety and depression. This new way of thinking and behaving carves new pathways in the brain. We deepen our faith in our god nature each time we are able to do this.

If we lose integrity with our true nature, we are forced to assume a false identity. That false identity is comprised of all the faulty beliefs from our childhood, those old tapes that get played repeatedly whenever we are triggered by an incident that robotically drives us into fragmentation. Both the behaviors that we adopted to handle those painful thoughts and the thoughts themselves become our assumed identity. Whatever thoughts we hold propel us to seek evidence in our lives that will substantiate those core beliefs. These thoughts can include negative ones like, I'm defective, I'm not loveable, and I'm unimportant.

These are not the truth of who you are. They are what you learned was true, and now your conviction is so strong that you attract people and situations into your life to validate those thoughts about yourself. This whole process is what I refer to as "going unconscious." You are not in your core but in your head. You're not in your wholeness. You're in a fragmented state, feeling separate from your core self, which means you are in need of Transformational CPR to bring you to consciousness.

Awakening the heart and breathing deeply allows us to feel the authenticity of our natural and grounded self. It breaks the confines of limiting beliefs and sabotaging behaviors that are not who we are. It's no different than passing out and losing consciousness. The difference when you literally pass out is someone hopefully notices and calls for help. If you're lucky, the paramedics perform CPR to initiate consciousness. They get you breathing again and reactivate your heart.

We don't have the power to change others, nor do we have the power to change certain circumstances. However, we do have the power to change how we feel about things, how we judge others, and how we respond to situations. In every moment, we have a choice about how we feel. Every moment is another opportunity.

A Course in Miracles, a text that aims to assist its readers in achieving spiritual transformation, states clearly, "The course does not aim at teaching the meaning of love, for that is beyond what can be taught. It does aim, however, at removing the blocks to the awareness of love's presence, which is your natural inheritance. The opposite of love is fear, but what is all encompassing can have no opposite…Nothing real can be threatened. Nothing unreal exists."[1]

When we let fear take over, we have weakened our faith and lost touch with our infinite nature, which is pure love. When we choose love over fear, we strengthen our faith in infinite knowledge, aligning with our true nature.

The world of the finite is attractive to our ego. The ego's job is to want, to compare. It wants what it doesn't have, and even when it gets something, it will always want more. It's always judging. Letting the ego guide your life will only lead you down an endless path of suffering. As long as we buy into the illusion that our happiness lies in the world outside, the world of the finite, we

1. Helen Schucman, A Course in Miracles (New York: Viking), Introduction.

will continue to feel heartache and disappointment.

We have all been taught that fulfillment is out there somewhere, in a relationship, in more money, in religion, in fame, success, beauty, and so on. How long are you going to let your ego run your life? The ego can only lead you down one path—the path of disillusionment and suffering.

Chapter 5
I Scream; You Scream;
We All Scream for Ice Cream

One hot summer day, when I was six years old and still longing for any kind of validation I could get, my sister's best friend Gretchen came to visit and I took the opportunity to get some attention. The fact that my parents were gone for three days meant that Gary, my sister's boyfriend, would soon be making an appearance. My sister was twelve years older than me, and I heard her complaining to my mom that she had to share a bedroom with her baby sister. "A girl my age needs privacy" she would say. I tried not to take this personally, but it was hard since I relished any moments I could get of my older sister's attention. She was very pretty, my sister, and was elected the prom queen of Beverly Hills High School that year. My grandmother once asked me in her harsh tone and Arabic accent, "Why aren't you as pretty as your sister?" I didn't quite know how to answer that question and still don't.

Gretchen and my sister looked alike. They had hair down to their waists, which they parted down the middle, and they wore long hippie skirts made of the softest cotton. Flip-flop sandals were all they wore on their feet in summertime. I was always barefoot. I didn't like wearing a shirt either, especially in summertime. My mom used to chase me around the house in her best attempt to keep me clothed.

Gretchen and my sister were outside in the backyard that afternoon smoking cigarettes and talking about boys again. Why do grown-ups like to smoke those awful things? I used to wonder. My sister always smoked when our parents were away. Regardless, it was a perfect day. The only reprieve from the sun was in the swimming pool. Besides, I was showing off my talent as a newly accomplished swimmer. My sister and Gretchen had given me swim lessons the previous year. Engrossed in conversation, they would obligingly applaud and tell me how well I was doing when I came up for air. I felt like a seal flapping its fins together, squeaking with excitement, and then diving down for my next trick, anticipating the applause that would soon follow. I half expected to have a fish thrown my way at any moment. I was invincible.

An hour of this game and Gretchen was ready to leave. She offered to take me for an ice cream, hoping to entice me away temporarily so my sister and Gary could have "private time," as my sister called it. Ice cream was all the encouragement I needed. I was out of the water, dressed, and ready, waiting outside like a puppy that had done a round of tricks and was waiting for her biscuit.

Gretchen drove an old powder blue 1966 Mustang with a white hardtop and leather interior. We hopped in and sped off in hot pursuit of some sugar. The ride to the shop seemed like an eternity, but we did arrive eventually. "Mocha almond fudge please!" That was my favorite. My second favorite was peppermint fudge ribbon. I guess I liked fudge because that was absolutely the only thing those two flavors had in common. We sat outside on the bench in front of the ice cream parlor and watched the people mill around like sheep as we licked the melting ice cream from our cones.

The ride home didn't have the same appeal, but I was with Gretchen, my sister's best friend, and that was cool. Halfway home, I was overheated and tried to roll down the window for some air. Oops. Wrong lever. It looked like the window lever, but it was the door handle. The door that I had been leaning on the whole ride home was flung open as we were moving fast down the busy highway, and out I fell. Not only did I fall out, I stupidly held on to the door for dear life, as if somehow, that might save me. If I'd still been in the water, perhaps that would have worked in my favor. The hard gravel was not nearly as kind on my exposed knees. By the time Gretchen could react to the horror she had just witnessed, my knees looked like the raw ground lamb called kibbe that my mother used to make. Gretchen slammed on the brakes, forcing the car to an abrupt halt.

We arrived back at the homestead, but there were no caretakers in sight. Damn! My parents were on another golf trip for the weekend. This was becoming a ritual with my parents being away on many weekends. Good for them. I guess after six kids, one needs vacation time, but why now, why this weekend, why in my hour of need? I got that my needs were unimportant. Once we were inside, my sister and her boyfriend snatched me up and rushed me into the bathroom. I didn't want Gary or my sister to help me. I wanted my mom. In spite of my wishes, they sat me on the counter over the bath room sink, blood bursting from both knees like a geyser. My sister ran to the kitchen to grab some alcohol. I knew this was going to hurt, so I yelled after her, "And some chocolate please!" She returned with the alcohol in one hand and my favorite Goofy mug in the other. As she handed me the blue plastic mug with the jagged little handle, she said, "Sorry no choco-late, but how's this?" I was disappointed that I couldn't distract myself with the sweetness of some creamy milk chocolate, but at least I had something to squeeze while the searing alcohol was doused over my knees.

I started to get the message.

> 1. The world is an unsafe place. Perhaps I had better protect myself a bit more.
> 2. Not everyone can be trusted to show up when I need him or her. I better learn to rely on myself.
> 3. Most important, not everyone carries chocolate when I need it.

I was formulating the belief systems that would eventually become my future programming. Cause and effect—certain beliefs caused me to make specific decisions, propelling me to take certain actions, producing distinct results, thereby creating my experience for many years to come. Negative beliefs can easily shape an undesirable future. Self-destructive thoughts arise in insidious ways, clouding our vision and dictating our experience, until we gain awareness about our deep-seated beliefs.

Denial runs thick. It keeps us from using our awareness to manifest positive changes. Disavowing our feelings has its place, but at some point, we must process emotions that accompany even life's most painful tragedies. Renouncing our feelings can temporarily keep us from grieving, but it can also keep us stuck in injurious patterns. When we aren't conscious of the undermining beliefs we hold, we have no ability to change how those beliefs impact our lives. The sabotaging actions we take because of certain core beliefs will remain habitual until we can observe them honestly and begin making different choices. New and unfamiliar behaviors create new grooves in the brain. All habits are hard to break simply because we have become accustomed to them and they provide a level of comfort and familiarity. When those tendencies begin destroying everything potentially good in our lives, we feel motivated to change. Over time, self-destructive habits can stop providing even a secondary gain, but it can still be difficult to change our old ways. Instilling new behaviors requires that we learn healthy skills to replace the old one. Overtime, the new behavior will take root and command dominion over the old, but it takes time and diligence.

In some cases, we have to hit rock bottom in order to wake up. If we performed Transformational CPR, before we lost everything, we would become present once again and line up with our infinite nature, which would guide us in a positive direction. Taking a new course of action, while guided from our true self, will align us with our life purpose. Shifting our thinking and our old behaviors can open the way to the miracles life has in store for us. Instead, many of us choose to stay asleep, walking through our lives in a slumber and wondering what happened. *How did we get to be this age?* We wonder why we can't achieve fulfillment in our lives. But it is our responsibility to wake up to the loving presence inside so we can fulfill our mission here. Many of us shrug off responsibility and blame others for our unhappiness.

It's easy to blame your partner, your parents, or your boss. Anything can be used as a distraction when done in an unconscious way. If we don't use what's presented to us, in the manner in which it was intended, we suffer unnecessarily and miss the opportunity to self-actualize. Relationships are a mirror if we are willing to see our reflection. Have you ever noticed how the things that bother you most about someone else, are the same things you dislike about yourself? That's hard to admit, but once you are willing to stop blaming those around you and look at yourself, the power to change is more likely to develop. When there is no one to blame but yourself for your current state, you have the power and the desire to change your life. When you are willing to take responsibility for your state of being, you will stop waiting for someone else to change in order for you to feel joy or peace. You can feel joy and peace right now.

Unfortunately, I had a lot of suffering to do before I learned this simple truth. I was still blaming others for my pain. I was still seeking acceptance and love from outside myself. I was completely dependent on others to feel validated. Without that authentication, I was in a perpetual state of agony.

Chapter 6
First Love

The subject tonight is Love
and for tomorrow night as well,
as a matter of fact I know of no better
topic for us to discuss until we all die!
—Hafiz

Jonas, my first love, created so much despair in my life, I was forced to my knees, praying to be released from my anguish. I met Jonas when I was fourteen years old. It had all the components of that clichéd first puppy love. He was incredibly handsome. My crush was instantaneous; unfortunately, every female in our freshman class shared my infatuation. He stood six feet tall with broad shoulders and a slim waistline. His olive skin set his green eyes off the way black velvet brings out the shiny green sparkle of an emerald.

One day, on our favorite hike, we found a hollowed-out water tower and installed a door we could latch from inside. It was our clubhouse in the woods. Trying to make it as homey as possible, we constructed a cot from wood and foam. We brought in beach chairs for the lounge area and secured a boom box with all our favorite music. I smuggled in candles whenever possible to make it a romantic spot where we wouldn't be discovered. It was our secret hideaway, a place where I shared my deepest secrets with Jonas.

When we weren't hiking in the woods, we were at the beach sunbathing and bodysurfing. We spent hours laughing, playing, and boogie boarding until the sun went down. We would exhaust our bodies completely before crashing out. It was heaven. Jonas was my best friend. I could tell him anything and not feel judged. He was my first love.

Everything seemed perfect. I could feel my heart bursting open. I thought this must be what it feels like to trust someone completely, to love and be loved without protecting myself.

Then it all came crashing down on me. Chatting with some friends in front of school one day, I learned Jonas had fooled around with a girl at his new job at 31 Flavors Ice Cream Parlour. I wondered just how many flavors it would take to fill him up. This was not just a girl; she was also his manager and an older woman. I was devastated. I could hear my friends speaking as if from a great distance. "Maya, Maya, are you all right?" I was thinking, Of course I'm not all right. But all I could muster was, "Yeah, I'm fine."

I couldn't imagine why he needed to court another woman when we were so happy. Wasn't I enough? Wasn't what we shared engaging to him? I felt betrayed. Obviously, it was not my first experience with betrayal, but this one had a particularly poignant sting. Just when I thought I had found love again, it was being ripped away. So here came the new question—not how do I find love, but once I have found love, how can I hold onto it?

What I was too naïve to understand at that time in my life was that if we have had early experiences of betrayal, we can typically expect to attract more deception into our lives until we heal the original wounds. We continue to find things that validate our beliefs even when they don't serve us.

I hadn't healed any of those early wounds. I was too afraid to acknowledge them. I did everything I could to avoid dealing with the painful events of my life. I was under the impression that if I neglected the feelings they would go away. If I expressed deep upset, it made my mother incredibly anxious. To avoid upsetting her, I learned to stuff my feelings. I wasn't sure if I was protecting my mother or myself, but it didn't matter. What mattered was that I still couldn't be honest enough to express my feelings. It was unsafe. With my father, if I expressed vulnerability of any kind, I felt shamed by him. His inability to deal with his own feelings made it impossible for him to do anything but shame us for ours. This style assured him he wouldn't invite that discomfort. I assumed if I kept busy enough, I wouldn't have to stop and feel. I learned, by example, to emulate the members of my family.

The heart is similar to the body when it comes to healing. When we fall down and cut our knees, the way I had several years ago, the body goes to work instantly trying to repair itself. The human body is amazing. The heart does the same. The earliest hurts take place, and the heart instantly goes to work trying to repair itself from the ache, if we allow it. I learned to deny the pain from such an early age that I had no skills to address sorrow or loss.

The coping skill I learned to replace being vulnerable was to shut down and hide my feelings and to act strong and capable. Most of us are conditioned from an early age to avoid what doesn't feel good and to grasp on to what does. We continue to lure in situations and people who trigger those old wounds to expedite the healing process.

Unfortunately, I wasn't learning fast enough and continued to attract betrayal over and over again. When would I learn? "Maybe when you start to get honest," a voice in my head answered. I wasn't expecting an answer and certainly not this one. I chose to ignore it and move on.

I ended my relationship with Jonas soon after. I moved on—or so I thought. I met someone else and promptly began a new relationship. Without any awareness, I had replaced one lover with the next to avoid any feelings of discomfort. I didn't know how to grieve. As long as I kept moving fast, I thought I would survive. I had plenty of friends and activities to keep me distracted. My rigorous fitness-training program was assurance of escaping any downtime. If I wasn't in training for a triathlon, I was running a marathon that would consume me both mentally and physically. The objective was to keep my mind and body so busy that I didn't have to deal with my feelings.

Chapter 7
Sherry's House

Most of my high school days were spent loitering at my best friend's house. Sherry's family was the opposite of mine. Her parents were divorced, Jewish, and Democrats. My parents were Catholic, Republican, and had been married for forty years. Sherry lived with her mom, Dede, and her older sister, Dana. Dede went to school to become an aesthetician once she and her husband divorced. She was an independent, feisty woman employed by an elite cosmetic line in Beverly Hills.

On Friday evenings, the Hill family would celebrate

Shabbat, a Jewish tradition commencing Friday evening and ending at sundown Saturday evening. Dede said, "Friday night was the eve of the day of rest." Dinner was the reward after candles were lit and prayers were said. I don't know what it was about the prayers that always made my heart feel full. The prayers were said in Hebrew, of which I didn't understand a word, but somehow that didn't matter. Words like Adonai and Elohim had a deep resonance that made me want to discover more. Later, I found these words signified God or Spirit. Just the sound of the words seemed to elicit a response in my body that I couldn't explain. A strange calm took over when I uttered the words or heard them spoken aloud.

My cousin Jon and I were forced into Catechism when we were young, which is like Sunday school in the Catholic tradition. Every Sunday, we would be dropped off at Good Shepherd Church, where we studied the Bible and learned about Catholicism. We sat in the chapel and went through our Hail Marys and Our Fathers. The classes were designed to prepare us for our first Holy Communion, which felt like being knighted. It was a graduation of sorts; relatives were invited to celebrate your rite of passage. After the ceremony, the relatives would be invited to our home for food and wine. The one thing I could always count on at our family gatherings was an enormous amount of delicious food. Prayers were said in my house, but were very different from how they were in Sherry's house. At dinner with guests or on holidays, someone would be asked to lead us in a blessing, but it was always the same stilted prayer that made me feel nothing. "Bless us, O Lord, for these thy gifts, which we are about to receive from your bounty through Christ, our Lord". The traditional Christian and Roman Catholic prayer before meals was recited in our home each time, but lacked gravitas.

I liked approaching the altar to receive Communion. At the end of church services on Sunday mornings, the priest would greet each person, look him or her in the eyes, and say, "Body of Christ" after dipping the mini-wafer in the chalice of wine. Then I would say, "Amen," at which point he would drop the litle, round wine-soaked wafer on my outstretched tongue. I would immediately return to my seat in the pews, get on my knees, and recite my prayers while the small wafer slowly disintegrated on my tongue. *Was the body disintegrating? Or was it just my thoughts about the body?* Either way, it always got me thinking. Even though the wafer didn't last forever, I was aware that something deep inside me was forever and I could feel it when I was in prayer.

Sherry's mom cooked a different dinner each Friday night, so I got to sample a variety of Jewish food, like matzo ball soup and noodle kugel, which is like Jewish lasagna, hold the tomato sauce, hold the cheese, and add some raisins to sweeten it. Shabbat was a night with family, at the end of the week, designed to give us a conscious break from the material world. It was an opportunity to be reflective and prayerful among loved ones. I always enjoyed this ritual. It gave me the chance to look inside and count my blessings. There was a lot to be grateful for, and sometimes I would forget that. Sherry's mom felt it was important to keep the tradition going in order to keep the family close.

This clashed with my father's version of family time, which meant gathering around the television set in the den after dinner. I hated television and found no connection at all with the members of my family during his ritual. I chose to be on the telephone connecting with my friends instead. My father couldn't understand why I didn't want to be a part of his customary evenings, and I didn't know how to communicate my feelings to him. He used to say to us, "Blood is thicker than water. Friends come and go, but your family is always your family." If he had acted more like a "customary" father by showing up to graduations and birthdays, his words may have had more impact. Perhaps if I had felt safe to ask him for help on homework or an explanation of something I didn't understand without fearing his rejection, I might have felt differently, but he didn't want to bother with that sort of stuff. It seemed to enrage him, and eventually, I stopped asking. I stopped expecting, but I never stopped hoping. The love that I had wanted from my father, I attempted to get from Jonas, Sherry, and other people in my life. I still hadn't found love, but I hadn't given up either. I knew that it was my desperate searching that perpetuated my misery, but I couldn't quit. I was addicted to motion and terrified of stillness.

My close-knit ties with Sherry's family and my absence from my own home upset my father, who gave me the cold shoulder upon my return. The house felt immediately unwelcoming when I entered through the door. My father would be sitting in his overstuffed chair, like Archie Bunker, in front of the television set. The tension inside was thick as mortar, and I couldn't wait to sludge my way past the family room to my bedroom, where I was protected in the concrete illusion of safety. Once behind the door of my chambers, I felt safe. I could talk on the phone to friends and feel connected, but my father would find a reason to start antagonizing someone in the family until his anger finally spewed out. He used to say to me, "What do you think this is—a hotel or something?" He had a problem with my being gone two nights consecutively. This created an internal belief of my being a bad person and having done something wrong. Those early beliefs are hard to break.

At the dinner table, Dad would often start an argument. If he came home in a bad mood, someone in the family would be the target. I tried to be invisible, hoping it would be someone other than me. I grew up waiting, watching, and dodging the angry outbursts I anticipated. Our imagination of what might happen is usually far worse than what actually happens.

I spent most of my preteen and teenage years in my bedroom on the telephone on weeknights. That was where I was getting love and validation, and I was desperately hanging on as if it were a life raft in a giant sea. Throughout my teenage years, connection was the priority. I didn't like being alone; it frightened me.

My friends were the closest things I had to a safety net during this time. They offered an ilusory feeling of belonging in a world where I felt alone. It was a temporary Band-Aid, a place where I was part of something at least. I could talk about my feelings somewhat, things that hurt or confused me, but still found it impossible to be totally vulnerable and authentic with my feelings. I wasn't able to express myself at home, which contributed to my isolation. It was difficult to let anyone see what was going on inside since I wasn't sure what I was feeling.

I discovered athletics at a young age and that brought me swells of accomplishment. I was a natural athlete, dedicating myself to fitness and health, ruled by the frenetic existential march, which ensured my busyness, leaving little time to examine my interior world.

When I was alone, anxiety would surface, attempting to get my attention, but I wasn't willing to listen. I had avoided my feelings for years. *What if they swallowed me up? What if I fell into a dark hole of depression and couldn't get out?* It seemed easier to put a lid on my anger and grief and keep busy.

My addiction to relationships assuaged my terror of being alone. The meaning of addiction is the use of anything, substance or otherwise, as a way of avoiding feelings. It's a way of focusing outward rather than inward, using a substance of choice as a way to check out of reality. One relationship bled into the next for several years, until it became one long, continuous relationship.

Chapter 8
C for Consciousness

I've chosen the word consciousness to represent the C in CPR. The first step in any CPR routine is to take the pulse of the victim, checking for responsiveness. I often feel the need to take my own pulse to check for places where I have gone to sleep, places where I have been in denial. I search for a deadening in my body, tension in my muscles, fatigue, shallow breathing, or plain old anxiety. If I recognize when I check out, I can prevent sabotaging behaviors that typically ensue. "Splitting off" is a style of coping that many of us learned to replace facing painful emotions that emerge. This skill becomes automatic over time. When we gain awareness around it, we create choices. We can space out while acting out old negative behaviors, or we can choose to stay present and put new, healthy coping skills that aren't destructive into action.

Habits develop out of repetition. We're capable of adopting a new habit just as easily as we created the old habit. As we choose a new way of managing our emotions, over time, the new behavior becomes more natural, but we must remain conscious in order to instill the new action each time, until it becomes automatic. Neurons that haven't been fired in years suddenly come alive and activate the part of the brain that has been dormant. It's especially difficult to react differently if we've been severely triggered and have become frozen and fragmented by an old injury. The process of undoing old behaviors requires mindfulness, pause, and diligence, but with patience and compassion, the new habit will trump the old one. The latest research in neuroscience has proven that we can create new neuro-pathways in the brain that will literally take dominion over the old ones.

The impulse to leave our body is alluring for many of us who assume something will be painful. We stop breathing and tense our muscles. We physically prepare for the discomfort so we can escape it, but we create more pain by resisting our feelings. Notice when getting a massage, how we often tense when our therapist finds a stubborn knot, creating more tension and agitation, but when we breathe and relax into the massage, the knot begins to loosen and we feel relief. It's a similar process emotionally. We can dissolve stress by surrendering, but when we resist whatever feelings present themselves, the temptation to act out in some way that is unhealthy to mind, body, and psyche is impossible to deny. Picture the little girl or boy inside of you who is calling to get your attention. All he or she wants is to be seen and heard. That child wants his or her feelings acknowledged, and if you continue to ignore that little kid, the voice gets louder and louder. The body will speak to us in the only language it knows, which is to break down over time. Those of us who didn't get seen and heard by our parents are the ones who tend to ignore our inner child. It's a learned behavior that doesn't have to be repeated if we remain aware and make a different choice.

Over time, the body becomes a pressure cooker of unacknowledged feelings. The resulting anxiety and depression become unbearable. It's just a matter of time before the steam from the pressure cooker must escape. Instead of being honest about our feelings, for example, we might say something hurtful (passive aggressive) to distance people we care about or become irritable and take it out on someone inappropriately. Perhaps we'll blow up at work, or maybe we won't speak up but shove our feelings down further instead, which will lead to depression. Neither of these options is satisfying.

Being an honest witness to your life is more empowering than playing the victim. We must remain present to our feelings and allow our resentments to dissolve or our lives will begin to unravel. We cannot be in the moment and angry about something that already happened or be worrying about the future simultaneously. You, and those around you, will suffer if you refuse to acknowledge your feelings.

Carrying resentments against anyone, including yourself, creates tension in the body and holds you captive. You have the full capacity to be free, happy, and in love. This unspeakable core of silent, awake awareness is always free; it's already at peace, but the mind simply must surrender to its presence. The body must melt into it, and then the world can be experienced fresh as it truly is.

Denial, over time, is problematic for a number of reasons. It forces us into a fragmented state, preventing any connection to our aliveness. While fragmented, we are denied access to our core, creating feelings of isolation, fear, anxiety, and depression. We are unable to make good decisions when we are disconnected because we can't hear the still, small voice inside that is always our guiding light. Although checking out appears to shield us from immediate pain, it prevents us access to the love and joy inside.

In order to protect our, fragile emotional state, we deaden our bodies, cutting ourselves off from our vitality, joy, and sexuality. We tighten the muscles in our body to avoid feeling anything. You won't feel anything but depression over time. No sharp pain perhaps but no joy either. We make unnecessary mistakes when fragmented, for example, getting in a fender bender, locking ourselves out of our car, arguing with loved ones, double-booking appointments, or getting sick, to name a few.

If I deny what I already have and already am, I automatically feel dis-ease, experienced as a discomfort in the body and an agitation in the mind. When I hold an expectation or judgment of another person, I imprison myself. By simply having the awareness that we are stuck in the past or future, it forces us to become instantly present. As in meditation, we have thoughts that filter in and out, but we acknowledge the thought and release it. If we do not engage the thought, it will dissipate and we will be able to guide our awareness back to the breath. Meditation teaches the mind to focus on what we choose rather than allowing it to wander aimlessly.

It's impossible to be present and worry about what may happen tomorrow simultaneously. If I am distraught over something, it's because I'm allowing my mind to wander back in time or creep forward. Stories are generated in our minds around an event or person that may or may not be true. If I adhere to an expectation or become attached to a specific outcome, it's detrimental because it sets me up for disappointment. The first step in Transformational CPR requires that we become completely honest and aware of our feelings. It's stated in the Bible, "The truth shall make you free." John 8:32 (NIV) Absolute honesty in any given moment invokes consciousness and immediately sets us up for a more positive outcome.

It's often our conditioning that entraps us and propels us into unconsciousness. It blinds us from the truth of who we are. So many of us are conditioned to search for happiness in the perfect relationship or the ideal job or the right amount of money, but nothing will ever be enough. Nothing can satisfy the ego's need for gratification. It is the ego's job to attempt to replace God. Once we have something, it's inevitable that we will want more. When we are pleased with our achievements, the temptation to want bigger and better beckons us. If not bigger and better, we want it to last forever. Inherent in that attachment is the heartbreak that comes when it's gone. What we have will eventually change. Everything evolves. It is the natural ebb and flow of existence. If we rely on outside circumstances for our peace and fulfillment, we will constantly be disappointed. We must be willing to wake up to the truth and be grateful for what we have now without any attachment to it. With attachment comes a gripping. Gripping creates stress and tension. Happiness is who we are at our core, but if we contract and hold on physically or emotionally, we can't experience that joy. Nothing outside can bring everlasting peace, only temporary fulfillment. True fulfillment is the nature of who we are, but we have to be in the here and now to experience it fully.

The ego wants to be right at all costs. It has no investment in protecting us. The ego mind will deplete us if we succumb to its circuitous wanting, and yet, its job is all about wanting. The ego survives on strokes. The more accolades, the stronger its force becomes, building us a false sense of self-importance. We can't eradicate the ego, nor would we want to, but awareness of the imbalance it can create is sufficient to change that dynamic and bring us back into a state of balance.

During a disagreement with a loved one, the need to be right can take precedence over creating a harmonious outcome. No matter how angry it makes us, we often need to prove our point. We need the validation, convinced another person's point of view is imperative to our sense of well-being. The ego desperately needs the gratification of feeling seen and heard, but at what cost? Once we are able to value harmony over being right, we end the war.

When the truth becomes more important than being right, looking good, or being liked, we recognize freedom as our choice. When I truly understood this and experienced it at the most profound level, my life began to change dramatically. I now practice forgiveness on a regular basis, not only for the people who have hurt me, but also for myself. I accept that I do the best I can with the given amount of wisdom and consciousness I have at any given time. I strive to improve, but it's imperative to accept the mistakes I have made here and now in order to move forward.

We are constantly teaching others how to treat us, whether we know it or not. People watch how we treat ourselves and in turn treat us in a similar fashion. If we don't respect ourselves, we can't possibly expect others to treat us respectfully.

Validating myself rather than expecting accolades from others, allows me to stay present and not give my power away. Thoughts about the past or the future hold no relevance in the present. After a string of negative thoughts occur, it's natural to have certain feelings evoked, such as anger, frustration, or sadness. Using self-awareness and rising above the attachment and identification to the story we've created, we can stop the self-perpetuated suffering. Awareness is the key to freedom.

Being conscious entails becoming aware of our

beliefs, thoughts, and behaviors. It requires raising our self-awareness and taking responsibility for our actions and how they impact others. The first step in the CPR process involves taking inventory. If you are suffering, you are in need of CPR. Your pulse is probably weak, your body is tense and contracted, and your breathing is shallow. If you are suffering, trust that you are manufacturing a story in your mind that has no relevance in the present. You are caught in a false belief or expectation. It's important to notice what story you're holding onto, whether it be guilt or regret about a past event or anxiety and fear about the future. It's imperative to catch yourself clutching a sabotaging thought from your past or future. Write it down if necessary. Keep writing until you can get to the heart of it. By having awareness of your attachment to a resentment, old belief, or expectation, you can reinvent your story and therefore change its outcome.

Once they become aware of their patterns, most people want to know immediately, "What do I do now?" It's critical to stop asking what to do and just sit in the awareness. Stay with not knowing and see where it takes you. If not knowing raises fear, which is common, be willing to sit with fear. Allow yourself to experience fear fully—not halfway but all the way. Now watch the stories that arise without engaging or judging them. Thoughts are a form of resistance that keep you from experiencing fear right now. Continue to allow the thoughts to fade and simply invite the feelings that are present. Be willing to immerse yourself for at least, one minute without any resistance. Meet your feelings completely. There is no way through fear or any emotion except right through the center. Feelings are temporary, like all things, and will pass if you give them your full attention. Once the feeling dissipates, you will be left with your authentic self; it was there all along, but you were too distracted by your thoughts to recognize it. Your authentic self is a state of well-being.

Raising one's self-awareness is a powerful step that can't be skipped over quickly and should not be under-estimated. Trust that you will be guided in what to do or what to say in any situation when you are present and in your core, which I will discuss in steps 2 and 3 of CPR. For now, stay in the awareness and be willing to see where it takes you. If you can remain fully present in the heat of emotion, the "what to do" will come from an organic place. There is no road map that fits across the board. Trust that you will be guided from deep within because you will be able to hear the still, small voice inside that is always steering you in the perfect direction and will never take you off course.

PART TWO

The Second Step in CPR
(Presence—Mouth-to-Mouth:
Trying to Survive through Relationships)

Chapter 9
Addiction and Self-Betrayal

I was caught in an addictive cycle, fully aware of the negative consequences of my choices and yet unable to make different ones. It felt as though my midbrain had been hijacked. I knew that freedom lay on the other side, but I couldn't imagine how to get across the sea of monsters before me without being dragged under. My feeble attempt to keep my head above water had always been to cling to relationships, and yet, I knew freedom would only come when I faced the demons alone and single-handedly. I continued to search for validation from the various partners in my life because

I had no clue about how to get that love from within. I didn't trust that I was good enough. Each relationship eventually led to the same discovery because I hadn't dealt with my own feelings of emptiness. After each honeymoon phase, the reality set in, leaving me disappointed and angry. On some level, I expected my partner to make me feel loved and accepted. Expectations are a huge burden to place on any relationship. No one could do my work for me; I knew that, but it didn't stop me from trying.

We all come to the precipice of our own psychological journey, better referred to as our dark night of the soul, but we must take that leap of faith and dive in if we want to experience true freedom. Peace is always a choice away, but it takes courage to meet our feelings. At any moment, we can choose to confront our fears, but most of us choose instead to ignore the arising feelings that constantly emerge. We betray ourselves by ignoring the internal call to self-actualize because we are afraid to take the necessary steps. Oftentimes, we realize that in order to free ourselves, we must make changes, and change is scary to most people. The only reason change is frightening is it's a break from the comfort of what we have always known, the familiar, even if it has caused nothing but heartache and pain.

When our soul is crying out to be freed and we ignore it, it creates a feeling of self-betrayal. We create an internal split by keeping ourselves busy and distracted. Some of us choose drugs or alcohol. Still others choose food, love, sex, work, or television-watching marathons. What you choose is irrelevant. Anything that leads us away from self-investigation keeps us in bondage. Truth is the only path that leads to total peace. When we hang our salvation on any outside circumstance to provide validation, love, or peace, we wind up disappointed. Things around us constantly shift and change. The idea that someone else or something else can provide peace is an illusion. The only real peace there is lies waiting for our recognition. It's always present. Why don't we pay attention to it? Why do we turn our backs? The answer is the same for most people: fear. It's the fear of paying attention, the fear of being present, the fear of being completely honest, and the fear of the unknown. And yet, the only thing that can liberate us requires confrontation of those fears.

I opted for immediate gratification, remaining a slave to

the intoxicating distractions around me at that time. There was an internal struggle occurring all the time, and it was tearing me apart. I knew what had to be done, but fear stood in the way while my resistance continued draining any self-esteem I had left. The terror was gripping, and I knew the monsters wouldn't leave me in peace until I confronted them. I hid behind numerous relationships, hoping one of them might finally slay my dragons, but each love affair culminated in my increasing disillusionment.

Chapter 10
Revolving Doors

The one relationship that continued to haunt me was my first one, which had ended so abruptly. Jonas and I had many breakups over the next several years. The theme of betrayal continued to emerge in my life. I caught Jonas in several lies in the years to come and got fed up with it. I had to force myself to move on while secretly wondering if we would end up back together.

I tried moving on, but there was never any closure with Jonas. The door remained open. This created a problem, since years and many relationships later, I considered reuniting with him yet again, but the timing was always off. When he was interested, I was involved with someone, and when I was ready, he was consumed in a love affair of his own.

This continued until one day when he met someone and I had a feeling it was substantial. I was relying only on my intuition for this information, but it felt accurate. Now I wanted him back and felt guilty about the way I had treated him.

I ran into Jonas and his girlfriend throughout every stage of their courtship. Either this was God's idea of a way to torture me for every evil thing I had ever done, or I simply had bad timing. The first in a series of events happened while I was driving down a busy boulevard in my neighborhood; as I turned a corner, I caught a glimpse of Jonas and his beloved standing on the corner nailing a sign into the telephone post. My stomach bottomed out. I knew this was a moving sale and that meant they were getting ready to cohabitate.

The next big event came on one particularly depressing evening. I was licking my wounds from a breakup with another boyfriend. We had just hung up the phone, finalizing any remains of a happily-ever-after. I was already feeling depressed when the telephone rang. It was my friend Roger, whom I hadn't spoken to for at least a year. Roger was tall and lanky; so thin he could disappear behind a telephone pole. He had more energy than five brand-new puppies. He was in town and wanted to meet for dinner. I warned him I was not the best company because of my recent breakup, but he insisted. I did everything shy of slapping myself to get up off the couch and out the door. I couldn't be bothered to change my clothes. I had been lounging around the house all day in a baggy sweater and a pair of old, faded jeans; I wore no makeup in case I started crying again, and my hair was a disheveled mess.

We met for dinner at a local restaurant a mile from my house, at his suggestion. Roger looked great and was sporting his usual spunk, like a greyhound dog at the gate, ready to race. We gave our name to the hostess, who informed us it would be an eternal wait for dinner. "Table" was always packed. People could usually be spotted crowding outside the door waiting with their brown-bagged bottle of wine. This was a "bring-your-own-booze" kind of place. There was one long table (hence the name) in the center of the restaurant; it was considered the community table and was shared by strangers and friends alike. There were two-tops and four-tops scattered throughout the remainder of the eating establishment. "First available," Roger answered the hostess before she could even get the question out. She smiled and marked us down on her clipboard list.

Thirty minutes later we were still waiting for our table when Jonas walked in, whistling, chipper as usual. (Of all the nights to run into him, when I looked and felt my absolute worst.) He instantly struck up a conversation with Roger, whom he hadn't seen in years. They were busy conversing while I stood there, invisible.

The last call I had made to Jonas was two weeks ago; it was a final attempt for some closure, since I couldn't put us to rest in my head. He was spilling into my dreams as well as my waking hours, until a close friend of mine finally said, "Why don't you just call him and put an end to your misery?" So I made the call, suggesting we meet for tea. We played a horrendous game of phone tag. He was evasive while replying to my phone messages. Tonight, I understood why. He had been dodging my calls instead of being honest about what was going on in his life. He couldn't close the door, which made it impossible for me to move on. I was giving him way too much power, and I knew it, but I felt helpless.

While in conversation with Roger, Jonas proceeded to disclose that he and his girlfriend had recently gotten engaged. How could he? He never once looked up at me or made any eye contact with me, as though I didn't exist. I quickly excused myself and bolted for the door. I wasn't prepared for the revolution that was taking place inside my stomach.

I puked so hard in the alley; I didn't know how I could possibly return for dinner. With mild composure and a forced smile, I reentered the restaurant, but Jonas was gone. He had grabbed his food and blew out the door, bringing food home for his soon-to-be wife, I imagined.

Roger took one look at my now-green face and grabbed my hand. "Why don't we skip dinner and go for a walk on the beach?" I nodded since that was the best I could do and followed him out the door. He had seen Jonas and me struggling like this for years. "You can't wait for him to get closure, sweetie. You need to create closure within yourself." He was right. Roger was so right. I was finally seeing it clearly.

We don't always get lucky enough to have closure with another person directly. In order to truly move on with our lives, we need to close certain chapters.

The Jonas chapter was one I needed to shut for good, but this time, I had no one to replace him immediately. I was terrified, jumping into the abyss of aloneness.

Chapter 11
Kickboxing

The final and most horrific hurdle to overcome with Jonas occurred within the year. I was shopping with my friend Annie. We were in giddy moods, drooling over bargains and ogling window displays. I always have fun with Annie. After several hours of shopping and walking, we had worked up an appetite and decided to stop for lunch. She insisted on treating me to lunch. Outside our favorite sushi bar, I ran into Jonas's sister-in-law, whom I had last seen ten years ago at her wedding party.

After formalities, she asked innocently, "Can you believe

Jonas is going to be a daddy? Isn't that great?" I had never been kicked in the stomach before, but I was certain that this was what it must feel like. I did everything I could to avoid falling to my knees, and it would not have been in an act of prayer. I don't remember what came next, but I excused myself abruptly to recover. I found the nearest bench inside and collapsed in a heap of sobs. I couldn't stop once it began. Annie rushed over and held me.

What hurt most was the sudden reminder of what I had carefully tucked away years before. Jonas and I had shared one intimate night in between romances. Within a month, I discovered I was pregnant. Horrified, but clear that neither of us was ready to be a parent, I made the only decision that made sense. I got rid of it. We were young, immature, and we couldn't make a commitment.

The day I had that abortion was the saddest day I can remember. I never told Jonas what happened. I was too scared of being rejected a second time. I had suffered through an abortion years before when we were a couple, and he was unable to show up then. I couldn't bear another slap in the face, so I kept it to myself. I never got to have his child or any child for that matter.

And he was now going to have a baby girl with his new love.

The next day, I enrolled in a kickboxing class. Kickboxing was not something I had planned on learning, but sometimes, life throws us an unexpected roundhouse and we have to be prepared to fight.

Chapter 12
The C Word

Two months later, my mother was diagnosed with breast cancer. I didn't know if I could go through this nightmare a second time. Ten years prior, she had been diagnosed with uterine cancer and was given a full hysterectomy. I was still trying to catch my breath from her first bout.

When I got the news that my mother had uterine cancer, I was in the middle of finals week at UCLA. Most of my time was spent at north campus, the school of theater, film, and television. I was almost done with my exams for the quarter, except for one final project. The night before my mother's surgery, I was in the editing room, desperately trying to finish cutting my short film. It was difficult to concentrate on anything but my mother's health. How did her cancer manage to eat away the lining of my stomach? I spent the night at my boyfriend Brian's house that night and cried all evening while he held me in his arms.

The doctors didn't waste any time. Western medicine seems to view infected organs as invasive, and the treatment plan always seems to be the same: remove the part. Remember when doctors would remove people's tonsils in cases of tonsillitis? Then they discovered that tonsils actually serve a purpose and that removing them was a bad idea. This did not instill confidence in the medical profession for me.

I got up and left Brian's in the same clothes I had been wearing the day before. I left without any sleep and without a shower or breakfast but stopped for a dozen red roses, as if roses were going to save my mother. I was on my way to see her before she would be carted off into the operating room where they would remove the parts of her that defined her womanhood. I arrived, parked my car, and rushed into the hospital lobby. My stomach was cramping, and I could barely breathe. I hurried to the front desk to ask where to find my mother, but I couldn't get the words out. I was all choked up. Once I gathered myself, I was directed to her room.

I wound my way through the hospital corridors, up and down elevators under awful fluorescent lighting. My heart was pounding, my head throbbing, and I still couldn't breathe. Room 503-C. There it was, right before me. All I had to do was enter. I hesitated and then burst through the door clutching my roses as if they were all I had left in the world. I stood there looking at my mother lying in that hospital bed in her silly gown. I hadn't noticed the trickle of blood that had made its way down my wrist, staining the sleeve of my blouse. I stood there bawling like a little baby, hardly cognizant of all the people surrounding her bedside. She tried to console me, assuring me she was going to be okay. I stayed with her as long as I could, not leaving until they came to take my mother away. It was time to perform the awful dissection.

My mom's last words to me as she was being wheeled down the corridor into surgery were, "Maya, please, don't marry him." She was referring to Brian, the one and only person helping me through this crisis. I knew she didn't like him, but her words came down on me with a crushing blow.

Now, ten years later, she was faced with cancer again, only this time, it was breast cancer and not so easy to get rid of. They couldn't just cut this one out or remove the entire breast. It had reached some of her lymph nodes. They were prescribing Tamoxifin, which is one step beneath radiation. She would have to remain on this toxic drug for five years. I'd heard about people who had seemed to recover from cancer, and just when everything appeared to be fine, the doctors discovered the cancer had metastasized and there was nothing they could do. I couldn't help wondering if my mother would be another victim on this list.

I hadn't prayed in years, but suddenly, I had this overwhelming desire to start again. I couldn't keep avoiding my feelings. I was too scared to stop but too tired to keep running. I was desperate, so I got on my knees and prayed, begging for guidance. I asked for the courage to face the challenges that were emerging in my life. I asked for peace to reveal itself now in my life. I had never had an experience of lasting peace. I'd had moments of peace during physical exercise or when I was out in nature and everything stilled for an instant, but before long, agitating thoughts would reemerge and I would dive into the ever-tempting distraction again. I kept hearing David Byrne singing, "This is not my beautiful life." I knew that a different life existed, but I needed direction.

Chapter 13
An Attempt at Peace

*My soul can find no staircase
to heaven unless it be through
earth's loveliness.*
—Michelangelo

My prayers were answered, but I didn't know how important it was to be specific when praying. My mother survived the breast cancer and even survived five years of prescribed poison. Although she experienced waves of nausea and caught every virus that erupted for the next few years, she lived. I worried about her since the poison had wiped out her immune system. I begged my mom to examine alternatives, but she was confident in her doctor. "Honey, the doctor knows what he is doing. He's a doctor," she would reply. I gave up trying, having come to the realization that my mother would never challenge Western medicine, much the same way she would never challenge Fox News.

I prayed for her to live through this ordeal and for her to be spared any undue pain and discomfort in the process. Unfortunately, I neglected to ask for peace in my relationship. I can understand my mother disliking Brian. Neither of my parents approved. He was fifteen years older than me and had long, straggly hair, pierced ears, and a ratty goatee. Brian was a beatnik artist and writer, who had practically led the sixties revolution, and I loved him. He was offbeat, not like the fraternity boys who surrounded me. He was worldly and erudite; exposing me to art, music, and subcultures I had known nothing about. As a working actor and writer, Brian was able to help me run lines and coached me on scenes for my acting class. I was learning about myself through him. It was the most exciting relationship I'd had.

Brian wasn't the type of guy my parents envisioned

for me, and I knew that. I didn't plan on marrying him, though I was expanding my mind. My mother walked into my bedroom one morning while I was in the shower. The timing was unfortunate because Brian and I had had a bad argument the night before and he was leaving a nasty message on my answering machine. He was livid as he hurled expletives.

My mother argued, "I don't care what the circumstances are. That is no way to talk to my daughter!" I had grown accustomed to such vulgar displays of his nasty temper. My dad had a similar way with words.

The main problem I had with Brian was his uncontrollable anger. After an outburst, he would inundate me with phone calls, letters, and gifts, apologizing profusely until I forgave him. It was an unhealthy pattern, and I knew it, but I couldn't dig my way out; I was hooked. Some people are addicted to alcohol or cocaine; I was addicted to Brian. When it was good, it was great. Our lovemaking was amazing, but after a blowout, it would take on a lethal urgency.

Things between Brian and me declined rapidly. I was unaware he was using cocaine on a regular basis, and it was spinning his jealousy into total paranoia. At first, I found his possessiveness attractive; it made me feel wanted, but it turned into an obsession and drove me away. A sideways glance from a stranger would send him into a rage, and I could usually be found hailing a cab or phoning a friend for a lift home. I swore each time would be the last.

I was being stalked wherever I went. Brian stationed himself outside my apartment, parked outside my work, and called me incessantly until he wore down my resistance and I picked up the phone. I was scared to leave him for fear of what he might do. He threatened to kill himself, swearing he couldn't live without me. He was crazy, and I was frightened. When I realized the severity of his drug problem, I found the strength to leave him. I told him if he didn't get into a rehabilitation program and clean up his act, he and I were finished for good. I refused to speak to him until he completed rehab. He entered a program immediately. I was relieved, knowing he couldn't follow or contact me.

Days later, my mother and I ventured into an art gallery. Steven, the gallery owner, was a handsome man, and he made his interest in me apparent. I explained my life was complicated, but he persisted until I agreed to a date.

One evening, we met for dinner. I told him about my crazy boyfriend and that it was impossible for me to get involved with anyone. He understood, disclosing that he was a member of Alcoholics Anonymous and he had been sober for three years. After dinner, I invited him up to my apartment for a cup of tea since we were having a great time. I often felt uncomfortable at home, having been stalked for the past several months, but another man in my place seemed to alleviate the threat.

Within an hour, there was a knock at my door. Certain it was Brian because of the furious pounding, I froze like peas. Steven wanted to reason with Brian, but I explained that Brian wasn't the reasoning type. Steven convinced me and prodded me into the bedroom while he headed toward the front door to confront the situation. I held my breath and waited.

I heard rumbling on the staircase, a huge thump, and lastly, the sound of glass shattering. I knew this wasn't good. Reluctantly, I picked up the phone to call the police, and the woman on the other end answered, "Nine-three-seven? Yes, we know, ma'am. A car is already on the way."

Obviously, one of my neighbors had responded at once.

I flung open the door and tore down the stairs. What I witnessed next was the catalyst for a huge turning point in my life. Shards of glass from my neighbor's window decorated the courtyard. Yards away, Brian had pinned Steven to the ground and was banging his head into the concrete in an attempt to change his mind. I looked at the violent scene before me and instantly knew that I had attracted this craziness into my life. I had been so busy blaming Brian and playing the victim that I had been unable to see my own part.

Barefoot, I ran over the glass like a yogi, without receiving a scratch or drawing any blood. I grabbed Steven's shirt collar, hoisted him off of Brian, shoved him upstairs, and slammed the door behind us. Where this strength came from I will never know, but I was grateful. I was tired of being the victim.

Steven's elbow had a gaping hole in it, revealing gravel, dirt, and mangled flesh. Draped over the bathroom sink, he watched the blood drain from his arm as I rinsed it. I grabbed a towel and desperately tried to stop the flood, but it was useless. Suddenly, my front door was busted down. The Santa Monica Police Department had ripped the bolts right out of the wall. They stood in the hall shining their flashlights and guns. "Step away from the sink and raise your arms in the air, now!" Stunned, Steven and I dropped everything, including the drenched towel, and raised our arms. We left a trail of blood as they forced us into the living room and shoved us onto the couch. After we were calm again and had wrapped Steven's arm, the barrage of questions from the cops began.

They encouraged us to press charges against Brian, reiterating how dangerous things had become. "If you press charges, it's a felony, since broken glass constitutes assault with a deadly weapon," they explained. My head was swimming, but still, I refused. We finished with the officers and were rapidly escorted to the nearest emergency room to attend to Steven's wound. The doctor stitched his arm as the sun rose up over the hills.

Chapter 14
Dr. Nelson

Ashamed of all that had transpired over the past few days, I unloaded on Annie with all the gory details. I knew how dangerous this game had become, and yet, I missed Brian. Annie handed me a business card from her wallet. "You need to call this woman. She can help you. She was instrumental in my getting through rough times with Jerry." I was desperate and willing to try almost anything. I called Dr. Joanne Nelson, PhD, the following morning and booked an appointment. I had never been in therapy before, but I decided now was a good time to start.

The sessions that ensued changed the course of my life. I was meeting with Dr. Nelson on a weekly basis. First, I had to learn how to tolerate my feelings and acknowledge whatever emotions arose during this period. I had some grieving to do. It felt like an impossible task since I had spent the bulk of my life running from all negatively perceived emotions. I was terrified, but I didn't have a choice. My crutch had been to use relationships to avoid my despair, and there was plenty of grief that had built up over the years. "The only way through the heartache is to feel the heartbreak," Dr. Nelson said. I knew she was right, but I dreaded hearing it. With her support, I felt confident that I could get through this. She represented the ideal "good mother."

I was hurting too much to allow diversions as substitutes any longer. Time was running out, and I knew it. Maybe it was a cumulative effect of the events of the past several years, but there was nowhere left to hide. I had insomnia, night sweats, and loss of appetite, all due to my terror of being alone. I had lost a considerable amount of weight. I imagined this is what withdrawal symptoms must feel like. *The only way through this hell is directly through the center of it,* Dr. Nelson's words came with a resounding echo. The difference this time was I had someone supporting me. She suggested I perform a letting-go ceremony, burning all the letters that Brian had written me. "It's time to say good-bye to Brian and thank him for all the lessons and time you shared. You need to get closure."

I spent the next few days indulging in my misery, sobbing for hours on end. I allowed myself to lose control completely, crying out loud without judgment. I screamed as hard as I could into my pillow, releasing my fear. I was outraged, grief-stricken, and scared, but more than that, I was relieved. I wrote in my journal every day in between my therapy sessions. Though I felt lousy for the next two months, I instinctively knew I was on the path to mending my broken heart. By indulging in this process, I knew I would be better off in the long run. Gradually, the pain subsided, and I felt better.

Out of nowhere came a gift from the universe. I had been working in entertainment, earning little money. Acting was my real passion, and I did as much local theater as I could. In between plays, I accepted employment from a director as his personal assistant, which parlayed into a job offer on his next film. The job would take me out of the country for four solid months. I was overjoyed. I would have several months to get over Brian without the fear of him appearing on my doorstep.

The only drawback in accepting the job offer was time away from Dr. Nelson. She and I were deeply entrenched in therapy, and it was helping. Dr. Nelson sent me abroad with a list of books to read, strongly recommending I write in my journal as much as possible. I spent the next four months in Fiji, working six days a week for long hours. I continued reading the books Dr. Nelson had given me and used my journal to stay in touch with my feelings. My main objective during this time was to carve out some quiet time at least once a day for self-reflection.

Chapter 15
Fiji

The flight to Fiji was incredibly long, and I was growing antsy. Once we arrived in Suva, the state capital, we debarked long enough to stretch our legs and walk a bit. The journey wasn't over though; we still had to get to Taveuni, a magical place known as the "Garden Island" for its lush beauty. Every bump and gust of wind could be felt from inside the cabin of the rickety aircraft. I was being tossed around like clothes in the spin cycle and wondered if this flight was a test run before the pilot got licensed. We eventually landed on what the Fijians called a tarmac. It was a strip of grass, half as long as the notoriously short runway on the island of Catalina. Even the most experienced pilot would admit this landing pad was daunting.

I was giddy with excitement by the time we disembarked the tiny airplane. It was a bright, sunny day, at 2:00 p.m. in this part of the world, and I had survived. We were greeted by a handful of smiling Fijians. The men grabbed our luggage, while the women welcomed us with a hug, adorning our necks with leis of freshly picked frangipani, a fragrant, indigenous flower. They showed us to our accommodations so we could settle in.

The house where I would be staying was a quick jaunt from the landing area. I opened the front door to my new home and was instantly charmed. The house was rustic, but had a stunning view of the lagoon. This would make a fine retreat house to heal my broken heart. In the bedroom, on top of the king-size pillow, lay a single frangipani picked from the garden out front. It created a fragrant aroma throughout the bedroom. I took a deep breath. My mind instantly conjured up thoughts and memories of Brian, but I forced myself to engage in conversation with the woman who was helping me get organized. I wanted to be present. I wasn't going to allow Brian to taint my tropical experience halfway around the globe. I would have time to write in my journal later, but right then, I was soaking up all the goodness from these fine people and their beautiful land. My only concern was that I might wake up from this dream at any moment.

The few of us who had arrived early were given two weeks of location scouting before the rest of the crew arrived, a great opportunity to explore the island. Fortunately, we had a driver who volunteered to take us around the island and teach us the lay of the land. There was only one road, and the island could be driven from one side to the other in five hours. Much of the film would be shot at sea in boats or on beaches around the island. Our crew was well equipped with drivers, whether at sea or on land. The film studio had employed a majority of the island dwellers.

I was certain the warm, bath-like waters of the South Pacific would wash away layers of sadness that I had accumulated, cleansing my soul, moving me from pain to purpose. The ocean was clear enough that I could see my feet while standing in neck-high water. The sea was abundant with psychedelically colored fish of every variety, and the temperature of the water was superb. I could swim all day and night and never get chilled. I learned to snorkel in these waters where I could spy on unfamiliar creatures of all kinds. Being so much a part of nature was the greatest healing agent. I was grateful to be here.

Taveuni is the third biggest island among the Fijian group. Unfortunately, most of the shoot was mistakenly scheduled on the rainy side, a minor slip-up by the producer. We had seventy-eight days of filming to complete our feature, but we battled conditions like weather, noise, and a sickness that was working its way through the crewmembers.

Dengue fever, hookworm, giardia, and a variety of other diseases infiltrated our army. I volunteered to fill in for the boom operator, second assistant camera operator, and the second assistant director as each went down—anything to keep myself occupied. I was also asked to substitute for the lead actress in underwater scenes without dialogue. It turned out she didn't swim well and we had similar measurements. All I had to do was wear a wig, covering my unruly, shoulder-length hair to emulate her waist-long, straight hair. I was so occupied I hardly had time to think about Brian, but I forced myself to process things in my journal in privacy.

The local paper had the same weather forecast every day, regardless of what was going on outside: "Sunny and clear skies" or "Mostly sunny with patchy clouds." Our only way to gauge the possibility of oncoming rain was to observe the cows. The locals told us, "If the cows are lying down, expect rain!" We didn't have much else to go by, so we relied on the local bovine population to predict our future. Each morning as we drove by the fields, we peered out the window to analyze the cows, fully aware of how insane this was but it proved to be reliable. Regardless, the landscape was mountainous, layered with lush forests, and surrounded by a crystal-clear, emerald-green ocean. I could grow accustomed to life on this island, I thought.

The Fijian people are hospitable, nurturing, and helpful, but they can't hold their alcohol. We discovered this on the film set, at the close of each day. After the martini shot (last shot of the day) was called, coolers of the local beer were hauled in as the grips broke down the set to prepare for the following day's schedule. After one beer, the locals were essentially useless. It wasn't uncommon to find them napping under a palm tree.

We had Sundays off, and I used those days to explore other islands and to discover the underwater world.

There was a lot to see under the surface of the water. On the surface, everything seemed calm and serene. Underneath, there were intricate castle-like coral reefs, iridescent but swarmed by an abundance of wildlife. The occasional shark could be spotted, touting his prey drive and putting everything in perspective; perhaps it was a reminder to stay on high alert and remain conscious at all times.

My first sighting of a shark sent electric shock waves through my entire body. I had two big fears in life: confronting my feelings and sharks. One of the boat drivers took us to a reef, far from the beach, to do some snorkeling on a Sunday afternoon. After motoring out several miles off shore, he cut the engine. "Here it is," he said. "What now? I'm supposed to jump out of the boat? Here?" I asked. Is he crazy? This water must be a hundred feet deep. What about sharks and things? I quivered at the thought. I was horrified, but didn't want to make a scene on our day off. I had never been in the ocean so far from shore. He referred to this spot as "Pandora's Box." I wondered what kind of jewels we were about to discover deep in Pandora's Box. Everyone else on the boat jumped in without hesitation; I tentatively followed.

Surprisingly, I discovered we were in shallow water, on top of a giant coral reef. In California, kelp beds grow from the bottom of the ocean bed like an underwater forest, but the ocean floor is hundreds of miles away. It was becoming clear to me that things are not what they appear to be, but fear keeps us bound; the avoidance of exploring what intimidates us only exacerbates the uneasiness. I remembered Dr. Nelson saying, "Whatever you resist will persist."

I was so engrossed in all the beautiful, multicolored fish I was encountering that I hardly noticed the thing that had everyone gawking. Halted in my own wake, I saw it. It was magnificent and graceful. How had I judged these creatures of God so harshly? Down at the bottom of the reef was a majestic white tip reef shark; it was my first run-in with a shark. It was close in proximity, but I was so in awe that I forgot to be scared. It was clear that this creature was king of the reef by the way he moved and commanded attention. I wasn't going to argue with him.

Once I climbed back in the boat, I was informed that

neither white- nor black tip reef sharks are interested in humans. They aren't dangerous, unless they are in a feeding frenzy and we get in the way. I suppose any animal can be dangerous when and if it is hungry, but we don't often hear of shark attacks by this particular species.

Ironically, the last three weeks of shooting, I was assigned to help underwater crew bait and photograph sharks. A lovely Australian couple had arrived from Sydney for this purpose, but they needed an assistant. They were well-known shark experts, and Ron was an underwater photographer as well. Val was engaging and full of life; she made it difficult to say no. *Hadn't anyone mentioned to them how deathly frightened I was of sharks?* Just because I had seen one three months earlier didn't mean the fear was gone. What if I saw a great white or a hammerhead?

Once I met the couple, I was immediately ashamed of my resistance. Their years of experience working with every type of shark imaginable, including the great white, had made them world famous. I remembered seeing the Aussie couple on television interacting with sharks from inside metal cages that had been lowered into the ocean. I was told they used metal suits while interfacing with great white sharks and Val had been bitten on her leg once but lived to tell the story. She had the scar to prove it.

Val was a pioneer, and we became fast friends. She was my mom away from home, taking me under her wing. One thing she said to me kept ringing in my ears, "It's usually the shark you don't see that will get you." You never know when that bit of information might come in handy. It was no accident that I was placed as Ron and Val's assistant. It was another opportunity to confront my fears.

When I accepted the job, I wasn't aware that my surface mind would be dismantled. The only explanation for my treading water in a shark-infested sea surrounded by coral that Val and I had speared with chum was that my soul was on fire. I was alive. I didn't allow my insecurities to rob me of this opportunity. Ron stood by, camera ready, waiting for sharks to photograph. This was crazy to my linear mind, but I was discovering the more I confronted my fears, the more they subsided and the greater the payoff was. Challenging my inhibitions blew open every corpuscle in my body.

Hoping these sharks were nonaggressive—or, at the

very least, had recently eaten—I stared as they approached us. We felt the vibration and saw the shadows encircling us, and that was my cue from Val to paddle back to the beach. I wanted to live to tell Dr. Nelson how well I was doing and how much she had helped me. I didn't realize that I could survive without Brian, but I was feeling more vibrant than ever. I wasn't ready to remove the respirator completely, but I was learning to love myself. I didn't need Brian to feel worthy.

Chapter 16
Who's the New Aussie Boy?

I managed to stay clear of any romantic pursuits until we were in the final stages of shooting, making a record high of six months since my last relationship. If it weren't for the tall, sexy Australian who showed up in the last three weeks, I might have managed another six months. Alex had landed a small role in the film as one of the bad guys.

His silky brown hair, piercing blue eyes, and olive skin all reminded me of Jonas. I have a weakness for men over six feet tall, and that he was. While I had been asking everyone about the bad boy with the sarong dangling from his waist who had magically appeared on set, he had been inquiring about the Italian girl in the cut-off shorts.

We got to know each other while working long days and soon discovered most of our impressions of each other had been wrong. He was not a bad guy, and I was not Italian. There was plenty of time between setups. We took long walks in the hills or along the beach at sunset. Sundays, our day off, we explored hidden parts of the island or went skin diving. Alex was a fish, having surfed since the age of four. He'd grown up in Perth, Australia, but moved to Sydney years earlier to open a fishing tackle shop. His sense of direction, whether in the mountains or out at sea, was incredible; Alex could find his way out of a tornado. I felt safe exploring with him, confident we would never get lost.

I decided to take time, after four solid months of shooting, to explore this part of the world. Ron and Val invited me to Sydney. They lived only a few subway stations from Alex. Things were complicated between Alex and me. Before he left Fiji, he informed me of his five-year relationship with a woman who was still living with him. He swore the relationship had been over for some time and disclosed that meeting me made him feel alive once again.

I didn't want to confuse matters and told him as soon as he sorted that relationship out to call me. I knew I still had work to do on myself in order to increase my chances of having a relationship while maintaining a sense of self.

During my three-week stay in Sydney, I was bombarded by phone calls and visits from Alex. In between dinner parties thrown in my honor, arranged helicopter rides, and a private plane journey to the capital Canberra, I was able to spend quality time with Alex. He lived in a busy district, close to Bondi Beach, a popular downtown area in Sydney cluttered with shops and restaurants.

Val invited me to Bali for a short visit and on to Papua New Guinea for a dive-boat cruise she was navigating. I gratefully accepted her offer, but when Alex found out, he showed up. Bali was his favorite vacation surf spot and a place he frequented. He promised me he had worked everything out with his ex-girlfriend and that she had moved out. He talked me into staying in Bali for three weeks while Val went on the dive boat without me.

It was in Bali that Alex and I bonded. My plans, prior to Alex's surprise visit, were to continue my travels through India, Nepal, and Thailand, but falling in love tends to change things. Alex showed me around the island and introduced me to a variety of people living there, both Balinese and American. Bali attracted many travelers because of its exotic land and rich culture; some of them even became residents. We rented a motorcycle since that seemed to be the easiest way to navigate the island. There were few traffic rules in downtown Bali. People ignored stop signs, and stoplights were a mere suggestion. I was thankful whenever we made it from one destination to the next.

One afternoon, Alex took me into the mountains of Ubud to meet his friend Terry. She was living in a beautiful palace, overlooking tiered rice paddies. Her place was completely open air with concrete floors throughout. When we rolled up, Terry was leaning against a pillar out front with a paintbrush dangling from her full lips, her rayon sundress blowing in the breeze. She was staring intently at the giant canvass before her, deliberating where to place the last-minute accents. Alex made our introduction and quickly vanished to relieve his bladder. A long silence ensued as we stared one another down. Her eyes bore into me with such intensity it sent a shiver down my spine. Attempting to divert her attention and break the silence, I complimented her painting.

After an eternity, I was relieved to see Alex come bouncing out to ease the awkwardness. He and Terry threw their arms around one another in a much-too-long embrace. There was something magnetic about her. I imagined most people were hypnotized by her physical beauty. She was a masterpiece creating masterful works of art. She had the most perfect nose I had ever seen; it was turned up at the tip ever so slightly. Her blue eyes and long dark hair were a stunning combination against her tanned skin. It was difficult to take my eyes off of her. I noticed all of her paintings stacked one on top of the other in her gallery as we made our way to the kitchen to have some sun tea. As the day progressed, I began to wonder just what the relationship between Terry and Alex might have been. Alex tried to convince me that Terry had had feelings for him some time ago, but they were not reciprocated and the two were now friends. Something in my gut told me otherwise.

The following day, Alex and I traveled across the island to Uluwatu, a famous surf spot. In a little surfboard rental hut, we were served cold drinks and munchies. Uluwatu was a magical place where the bluffs hung over the water's edge and craggy rocks created a provocative view from the top. I sat on the cliff sipping my coconut, watching Alex expertly surf the dynamic waves, and I quickly forgot about Terry and my jealousy. I wanted to forget.

The water in Bali is warm like in Fiji, and you can swim day or night. Alex and I spent many evenings playing in the waves. Our time in Bali was what I imagined a honeymoon to feel like. I couldn't have written a better script for myself. It was perfect.

Alex introduced me to the resplendent world of yoga. I quickly adopted yoga as a way of life. Once it entered my bloodstream, things began to shift in my life. It made me strive to be and do better, to treat myself with compassion. Since becoming more sensitive, I ate more healthily, and I treated others with kindness. We practiced yoga together every morning on the beach. Watching Alex practice was an inspiration. His long, lean muscles relished every asana (posture). I watched his glistening limbs elongate, while he infused them with the breath of life. Alex was trying to teach me how to breathe Ujai. It reminded me how my breath sounded underwater while scuba diving in Fiji. Breath combined with movement slows the mind down, making me feel alert and yet calm and centered. If I can remember to stay connected to my core, while growing and expanding, I can have an enriching, yet grounded experience. With that, I can remain centered and calm in the midst of change because I have a constant and that is myself to hold. The deeper my roots dug into the earth, the more I was able to reach, lengthen, and expand out like the branches of the tallest tree. Yoga was the bridge to all that I was practicing.

Balinese sunsets are cinematic in nature with every shade of orange, yellow, and red; they are too spectacular for words. We were staying in a bamboo hut just off the beach with an outdoor shower. The only downside of the open-air bamboo huts, as charming as they were, was the mosquitoes had free access. Mosquitoes love me. Alex and I started a ritual every evening just before dusk (mosquito hour) of lighting coils around our room to discourage the mosquitoes from entering. Our ritual didn't seem to dissuade them, but we continued with it anyway. My real savior was the giant white mosquito netting surrounding the bed. This was the one place the little critters couldn't get me.

Three weeks came to a close much too quickly, and Alex had to get back to his business in Sydney. He convinced me to give up my travels and go back with him. Love does things that no one can explain, so I agreed.

Once we were back in his apartment, things went downhill. The second day back, we were having breakfast at the kitchen table when I noticed pictures scattered everywhere of he and Emily, his former girlfriend. I tried not paying attention to the knot in my stomach, but it didn't stop there. Something didn't feel right. I didn't want to stay connected to my core right then. It was miserable. I wanted the feelings to go away and not ruin this perfect romance we were having.

After breakfast, I kissed Alex off to work and slipped into the shower. Once out of the shower, I quickly got dressed. Our summer is Australia's winter, and fall had set in since our return from Bali. I had nothing but summer cloth-ing with me. I rummaged through the closets, looking for something warm that might fit and found an entire woman's wardrobe—Emily's wardrobe. The impending doom, which I could no longer ignore, consumed me.

Alex had promised me that Emily had moved out a few months ago, which was the reason I had allowed myself to continue seeing him. It was too late to change that now. I was clearly invested in this relationship. Thoughts of revenge plagued me. A rage I hadn't felt in a long time welled up inside me. I could feel blood rush to my head and swell my brain. I felt stupid. I wasn't sure what to do next. I didn't want an explanation from Alex. I didn't want to hear that Aussie accent begging me to stay. I was so tired of lies and excuses from the men in my life. I was done making excuses. I called the airlines immediately and booked my flight home. I was on a plane heading home within three hours. As badly as I hurt inside, my taking action to take care of myself felt empowering. I was setting a boundary. Boundaries had been difficult for me in the past because I was afraid if I said no to someone, he or she would leave or get angry. I realized we're always teaching others how to treat us. If I wasn't respecting myself, how could I possibly expect someone else to respect me?

Chapter 17
Knocking on Grief's Door

Having been away from home for six months, I was relieved to be in my own apartment once again. It had been two weeks since my return from Sydney, and I was not responding to any of Alex's pleading phone calls. I decided I'd endured enough. I was choosing to love myself and to stay connected to my core, to honor and take care of the little girl inside. I would no longer abandon her in a time of need.

I caught a cold on the airplane and had been feeling dreadful for the past week. My chest was heavy. I made an appointment to see an acupuncturist. My cough was affecting my workouts and keeping me awake at night. Before my trip abroad, my fitness routine consisted of trail runs in the Santa Monica Mountains several times a week. I kept in shape while traveling by swimming, hiking, or running every day. Climbing the Santa Monica Mountains had never been easy, but these past few weeks, I was wheezing all the way up the mountain as if I were climbing Mount Everest. I couldn't understand why I felt so exhausted.

By the time I met with the acupuncturist, I was ill. This doctor of oriental medicine was Korean, and if I had known about the Korean approach to acupuncture, I might have thought twice before signing on the dotted line. He began his treatment by pricking every square inch on my chest with his tiny magic needles. Needles are one of my phobias, but I'd heard about the efficacy of acupuncture. He twisted each needle a bit deeper, until I cried out in pain, spurring him to turn the needle further. He sent me home with a tiny bag of herbs I was instruct-ed to take before bedtime every night until our next visit. I tried, but I couldn't stomach the taste. I boiled the herbs into tea. I froze the tea and attempted to drink it iced. I plugged my nose while drinking. It was no use. I couldn't get the herbs down my throat.

My cough persisted, and I got progressively worse. I couldn't continue any physical training, which irritated me. I wasn't going to let Alex, or any man, get me down anymore, but I was simply too taxed.

My sister raved about a doctor she had seen and suggested I call him. Motivated by my lack of sleep, I set an appointment with her doctor. Returning to the Korean acupuncturist was not an option. I got an appointment with the new doctor, but by that time, I was well into the beginning stages of walking pneumonia. My lungs had filled with fluid. I didn't know the first thing about pneumonia. Without warning, the doctor grabbed a large needle and injected me somewhere in the fleshy part of my rear. That shut me up. Still stunned, I was sent home with a strong round of antibiotics and no choice in the matter. "This can be a life-threatening illness if not properly treated," he warned me. "You must take the antibiotics and rest, if you want to get better."

I surrendered to my bed, obeying the doctor's orders so I could kick this thing. The illness took me down for two months. I was aware of the grief trying to surface, though

I was stubborn about surrendering to it. I copped out and watched movies, read books, and talked on the phone, neglecting to do the one thing I knew would heal me. My compulsion to run was still bigger than my need to evolve when it came to matters of the heart. I was more addicted to the instant payoff than the long-term gain. My dilemma was figuring out how to get to the other side without slaying the dragon.

Chapter 18
My Introduction to Buddhism

My sister, who was always into something new and exciting, was studying Buddhism. She invited me to attend a gathering one evening. She was concerned about my current state of mind and wanted to help. I was open and willing and considered myself a seeker at this point.

I had no idea what to expect from Buddhism, but I was so distraught after the numerous breakups that I accepted her invitation, wanting to try even if it proved to be just a distraction from my thoughts. I couldn't trust my mind. I was still torturing myself with thoughts of the past and wondering how to navigate the future. I felt hopeful that the introduction to Buddhism might be a path out of my misery.

Following the sound of people chanting in unison, I made my way through the obstacle course of empty shoes lining the walkway of the A-framed cottage in the canyon. Chills exploded up and down my spinal column, awakening every nerve in my body. I sat on the front step, absorbing the frequencies, allowing myself to be carried away, as my mind and body dissolved.

A woman approaching the front door roused me from my trance-like state. I stood up, removed my shoes, and entered the house. My sister looked up as I entered, a smile of relief on her face as she motioned me to take the empty cushion next to her. The chanting continued until an elderly man dressed in colorful robes brought an instantaneous hush to the room with his mere presence. The group dropped into deep meditation for the next twenty minutes without any words spoken. I had a hard time remaining still as I waited anxiously for something to happen. My curiosity made it impossible to keep my eyes shut. I couldn't resist the temptation to spy on the man in front, wondering if he was fidgeting like me, but he never flinched. He remained motionless with a penetrating serenity.

Finally, his gentle words pierced the silence. I extracted the juice I'd been thirsting for by squeezing each word. It was as though he were speaking directly to me. *How does he know what I'm going through? How does he know what I'm thinking?* I listened to the Buddhist monk speak about the mind and how we allow it to control our state of being. "Thoughts precipitate feelings, and if we are having negative thoughts, we are going to have negative feelings that follow," he said. Every sentence created the perfect narrative, easing my restless mind.

The meeting came to a close, and I was full. This alien feeling came from within rather than from outside of me. My curiosity was piqued. I thanked my sister profusely and inquired about the next meeting. I was relieved to find the meetings happened weekly. After the obligatory introductions and refreshments, I quickly excused myself. I couldn't wait to be alone. It was an unfamiliar feeling; I was alone and yet so full, with no fear and no anxiety.

Inspired by Buddhism, I was determined to start a

meditation practice. I didn't know how, but I wanted to quiet my mind and do more self-investigation. I had a feeling the path of self-introspection would lead me to my core.

Chapter 19
The Silent Monster

*Like a great starving beast
my body is quivering fixed on
the scent of light.*
— Hafiz

A few months and many meditations later, I was excruciatingly aware of the one common thread at all of our family gatherings. I have a large family, and it grew exponentially with boyfriends, girlfriends, and relatives joining. Our home was the place where all the waifs and strays would end up on holidays because they had nowhere else to go. Most of the gatherings revolved around food, but everyone was welcome. Regardless of the number of people who showed up, the common thread was the absence of silence. There were never any long pauses in conversation. It was almost as though there was an unspoken agreement among those who attended not to allow any pauses. It was the opposite of my meetings with the Buddhists in the canyon. Those meetings were infused with comfortable silence and blissful quiet.

I began to notice the lack of peacefulness in other places as well. It became a game I would play with myself. Everywhere I went, I would observe people and track their comfort level with presumed bouts of silence. I noticed a growing anxiety if the conversation came to a pause. It was as though stillness was the big, scary monster hiding in the corner that no one would confront.

What were we all so afraid of? What would happen if the gap were to be elongated for more than an instant? I noticed a growing agitation within me when a long pause emerged in conversation. My mind would quickly jump to what I could discuss; it didn't matter as long as the silence didn't win the game.

I started to refer to the gap as "the silent monster." Would it eat us alive? Would it annihilate us? What would happen if we allowed the silent monster into the room and didn't feel the need to hide or cover him? What if we made friends with the monster?

Nothing dark can hide in light. Light attracts more light, so why not turn on the lights and see if the monster goes away or if he even exists? Confronting the monster was nothing short of a big doorway into the center of my being. This was the home of my core self. This was it! This was the place I had been trying desperately to return to, but I didn't have the right road map. The stillness that I was beginning to embrace gave me access to inner peace. All I had to do was become present to what was there in any moment. I had the keys to the inner kingdom if I was willing to use them. From this place, everything was possible. In spite of this, I still wondered if I was brave enough to keep the lights on when confronted with some of the bigger issues facing me—the things I didn't want to look at, the not-so-beautiful things.

Chapter 20
Café Chocolate

I met my next boyfriend drinking tea at one of my favorite local hangouts. I spent the next three years trying to get him to love me. I had my nose buried in my writing when he casually walked into Café Chocolate, but I still managed to notice him immediately. Chris had dirty-blond hair and large blue eyes, and he smiled at me while at the counter waiting for someone to take his order. After placing his order, he sauntered over to visit.

We had met at Café Chocolate the year prior. He had been away on location, shooting his first feature film.

He asked me for my telephone number at our first encounter. "I thought I had lost your number, but I found the scribbled digits on a Café Chocolate napkin this morning and was provoked to come here today. I just got back in town," Chris explained. I recalled our first meeting. He had been sketching my portrait on a Café Chocolate napkin without my knowledge. I noticed the sketch as I slid by to use the bathroom. It was so realistic, but when I commented, he quickly scrunched up the napkin, dismissing his talent. I discovered he was multitalented but never boasted. He wrote math books for Harvard University, which he was embarrassed to reveal.

"Do you mind if I join you?" he asked. We sat and talked for hours. Several industry people at the film festivals he attended around the world had been courting him. His independent film had received attention from the press. This had sparked interest among agents and managers wanting to sign him on the spot, but he wouldn't commit to anyone.

Chris was non-committal in every arena of his life. I should have paid attention to the red flag. It's funny how most of us choose to ignore the surgeon general's warning even though it's clearly written on the side of the box. Before he left, we arranged a date. I was excited, although I was gun shy from my most recent escapade with Alex.

Our first official date was on Halloween. We had a blast that afternoon, creating original costumes out of things lying around my apartment. Chris was care free and spontaneous and never ran out of fresh ideas for play and having fun. We concocted photo shoots and created short films, spending hours in the editing room. We built things and designed art together. His childlike nature was highly developed, which inspired my little girl to play with joyous abandon. He was twice my size, enabling him to lift and twirl me, creating acrobatic maneuvers that entertained us for hours.

He had an eclectic group of friends comprised of writers, producers, directors, and actors. It was no accident I attracted someone like this at this time in my life. As long as he didn't lie and didn't cheat, he appeared to have some promise. At least that was what I thought at the time, but Chris had a problem with commitment. He couldn't commit to an agent, let alone a relationship, which was why his film career tanked. He assumed the offers he was getting for representation, as a writer/director, would always be there. He had no prior experience of how the film business operated in Los Angeles. When he was ready to sign with an agency, to sell his next screenplay, no one remembered him; the urgency to sign him had died. Hollywood has a short attention span. You're lucky if you are chosen to be the flavor of the month, but you better work it or you're gone from their memory banks.

Chris was traveling back and forth from Los Angeles to Santa Cruz in our last year together. He had given up his place in Los Angeles and was practically living out of his car while trying to sell his latest screenplay. No matter how hard he tried, he couldn't make it happen. He had several meetings lined up with major producers and studio heads, but in the end, no one was willing to put an offer on the table. He was running out of money and time. He felt too inadequate to make a commitment to our relationship. After three years, I finally put an end to it, with the realization that our relationship wasn't going anywhere. I was getting better at closing doors, but I was discouraged about the possibility of ever securing love in my life.

Chapter 21
Purple Haze

I saw Marcel at a friend's party one evening, and the moment we made eye contact, I knew he would be my next boyfriend. He had kind eyes, and I like that in a man. I had no idea what I was signing up for with Marcel, but being with him took my mind off Chris. Marcel introduced me to barefoot dancing, which I embraced immediately, dancing three nights a week. In this healing space, I could dump unnecessary baggage through movement and not be limited by words and thought forms. The only dancing I knew was done in nightclubs surrounded by loud, thumping music and cigarette smoke. This was alcohol-free dancing in workout attire—no makeup and no masks. Marcel watched me while I was lost in my dance; he shook his head in disbelief and commented, "Like a fish to water." Physical things had always come naturally to me.

There was always a fun activity going on around Marcel's pad. It was a giant flophouse, and you never knew whom you would run into while on the way to the toilet in the morning. A group of us would strap on rollerblades in the evening and blade through the streets to the dance hall like an urban gang. I felt like I had found a new family, and I was in need of family after my break with Chris.

What I hadn't considered was the abundance of drugs involved in this package deal. The group got loaded at Marcel's house before dancing. After dance, we invited friends back to the house to the Jacuzzi. We kept the party going until early morning. The partying seemed to extend from night into day and weekends into weekdays, but I felt a sense of belonging that I had always wanted. I didn't think there was any harm in our recreational fun, until I realized the drugs were Marcel's way of life.

I was afraid of being excluded from the activities that were taking place in the group of friends Marcel had introduced me to, but drugs were not part of my world; I was an athlete. Katrina, one of Marcel's best friends from Santa Cruz, was spending a lot of time with us. She was athletic, fun, and very sexy. She always gave me sound advice and had already done everything I wanted to do. I admired her confidence. She was a professor at UC Santa Cruz, teaching gender studies and English literature, obviously no dummy. She quickly became my best friend.

Four of us were practically living at Marcel's house. It was a giant slumber party all the time, quelling any fear I might have had of loneliness, but there was a serious price to pay, even through the amazing journey. I wasn't able to maintain my part-time job as a fitness instructor, eventually getting laid off. It was difficult getting to work on time because we were staying up too late.

Psychedelics were a big part of the tribe's experience. I had managed to escape drug use all through high school and college. I was far too involved in health and nutrition. Drugs would have compromised my fitness level, and I was too competitive to be slowed down. I realized psychedelics can teach many things in a very short time, allowing people to push beyond their limited thinking, allowing them perhaps, to explore things not otherwise possible because of early conditioning. After several months, I was in a haze. I had withdrawn from my family and friends; I wasn't doing anything to advance my career; and I had lost sight of my purpose. Things had gone too far.

My oldest brother (a lawyer) came to visit me one day. We took a long run on the beach followed by dinner. He expressed his concern for me, but I couldn't hear it at the time. I couldn't admit that I was having difficulty, because that would require me to make a change I was not ready to make.

The following weekend, Marcel and I were driving back from a music festival in Northern California. We had been camped out in the woods for the past four days with hippies from Santa Cruz, Marin County, and San Francisco listening to a fantastic lineup of popular, internationally renowned bands.

About two hours from home, we were pulled over by the highway patrol because we had neglected to turn off our high beams. When the officer approached the driver's-side window, his flashlight beam landed on Marcel's paraphernalia in the center console. That was all the ammunition he needed to drag us out of the car and search our vehicle. I looked over at Marcel, who was sweating profusely. I didn't understand what was wrong with him until the officer opened the trunk and searched our bags. Inside Marcel's duffel bag was a potpourri of drugs I had no idea he was carrying.

He looked at me and whispered, "I'm sorry." We were handcuffed and carted off to the Santa Barbara County Jail. I was placed in a tiny cell with concrete floors, a steel bench, a bacteria-infested toilet, and four other women. I couldn't imagine where they took Marcel.

Hours later, the metal slot in the door was opened and five brown paper bags were dumped into our holding cell. It didn't have the same appeal as Mom sending me off to school with my brown-bag lunch. I reluctantly opened one of the bags and emptied out the contents. The meal consisted of a small carton of homogenized milk, which I wouldn't drink, and a bologna sandwich on white bread, which I couldn't eat.

I lay down on the steel bench and tried to sleep it off,

hoping I would wake up and discover this was just a nightmare I was having. I eventually drifted off, only to be awakened by a screaming lunatic. It was the anorexic blond in our cell. She had gone ballistic, clawing at the door to get out, screaming at the top of her lungs like a wild animal in a fight for its life. I listened to her rage on for fifteen minutes, until I lost my cool and yelled for her to "shut the f--- up!" I had lost control, but she did stop screaming and I was grateful for the silence.

Eventually, I was given the obligatory phone call. With my tail between my legs, I called my brother (yes, the lawyer) to say, "Okay, you were right, but I need your help right now." Within a few hours, he was there to bail me out. "What about Marcel?" I asked. My brother reluctantly agreed to expedite Marcel's release. The drive home was silent. There was no point in "I told you so." We both knew what needed to be done.

I was tired of desperately seeking love from others. As long as I placed a higher value on getting validation from outside myself, I would continue to make bad choices in relationships. I was still addicted to the belief that I was unworthy, still believing underneath it all that I needed others to validate me. Like any habit, with repetition, it became second nature; however, my core remained intact. I knew I must stay connected to that. It was the only constant. My life had reached a low point, and it was up to me to make the shift. I had to recommit to staying present in my core each moment, and every moment was another invitation.

Chapter 22
P for Presence

The "P" in CPR stands for presence. Once we have established that we have fallen asleep, how do we regain consciousness? We established earlier that having the awareness that you're split off from your authentic self immediately creates the space in which to become more present. That step alone, although it may sound simplistic, does direct our attention to the moment before us. There is no way to be present unless we are in integrity and relinquishing resistance of any kind. The moment we tell a lie and betray ourselves, we typically move into denial, giving up our wholeness, and consciousness is lost.

I have labeled the P in CPR as presence. The second step in this process is a far more active step than the first. Step number two in any CPR manual is to perform mouth-to-mouth resuscitation in an attempt to create airflow where there hasn't been any. The most effective way to wake up is by breathing. It immediately drops us into our bodies and helps us become more alert. Animals, whether acting as prey or predator, experience increased breath and heart rate. When we are in a flight-or-fight response, much like animals in the wild, it forces us into total presence, ready to defend ourselves or to run from something, activating our sympathetic nervous system. The absence of breath removes any animation in the body, rendering it totally lifeless.

The moment we take a couple of deep breaths, we instantly become more relaxed and grounded in our bodies while simultaneously becoming more alert and aware of our surroundings. Take a few more deep breaths and look around. Colors may become brighter. Objects may shift into sharper focus. Take more breaths, and you might even feel emotions well up. Tears may be released if there is buried sadness. The breath will make way for whatever is present to surface. Notice how a few more breaths immediately gives us a sense that we are more grounded in our own bodies. We feel a greater sense of ourselves while the unnecessary things, such as stress and muscle tension, fall away. Armoring that has become rigid and stuck begins to loosen its grip.

If, for example, my spouse doesn't show up for my book signing or some other major event, based on my history with my father, I would most likely be triggered. Being triggered is nothing more than a current event catapulting us out of the present and into the past, traumatizing us once again. I become a little girl again and feel unimportant. I build a case and make meaning about my partner not showing up. *He doesn't care enough. He doesn't think I'm important. He should show up at important moments. It's his responsibility to know when to come through for me. He should know my sensitivities.* Each thought builds evidence to validate my earliest belief that I'm unimportant. Now, I'm no longer present; I'm totally fragmented by this one event, justified or not. The stories I create build unrealistic expectations of others. I'm now the victim, and the other person is the perpetrator. Our immediate reaction when we are wounded is often to blame someone else rather than own it as our own injury; in doing so, we relinquish any chance to feel whole again.

Triggers can be reminders to look inside first instead of lashing out and getting angry, blaming others and expecting them to fix it. I can remain stuck in my discomfort or I can transmute my pain into healing. I can step out of victimhood and stop attacking others, which will free me. It's important to be mindful of our judgments and expectations if we want to be released from total agony.

Not taking things personally instantly reduces stress and improves our relationships. We don't have a clue what is going on with other people, and it usually has nothing to do with us. The moment we get triggered by something another person says or does, we often attack the person because we see ourselves as being preyed upon. What would be more helpful is to call a timeout and write in our journal to find out what childhood pain of ours got activated. What old belief was stirred up inside? It's an opportunity to work through our stuff. Sometimes, we process the issue on our own and discover it's unnecessary to have any further discussion. Other times, we may find something left over that needs to be talked out with our mate; however, we will be more able to have a reasonable discussion when we feel grounded and present and not overly emotional. When we're not functioning from our childhood wound, we are rational and sane and are less likely to blame another person for our sensitivities.

It's impossible to have a productive conversation with someone when we are in a fragmented state. It's helpful to take responsibility for our part every time. It's tempting to blame others for making us angry or for letting us down, but we always have a responsibility in all situations, and unless we do our work, we lose the opportunity for growth. This doesn't mean the other person's actions are right, but it is an opportunity to heal old wounds. We must first look inside, even though it's compelling to confront the other person at the moment of injury. Those discussions that we engage in before doing our work always escalate because one or both people are fragmented. When we are fragmented or in our childhood wounds, we cannot listen to our partner. We attack and defend, getting nothing accomplished and saying damaging things, that we often regret. Our whole body shuts down, including our heart. We become protective and no longer present because we have shut off from our core.

We respond much the way we did as children during that past trauma. Trauma isn't always a huge accident, a natural disaster, or a physical injury. Trauma can be an emotional wound, like living with an alcoholic parent who was emotionally unavailable. Trauma isn't always one single event but can be repeated exposure to verbal abuse or neglect.

Getting present takes us out of fragmentation and moves us into our wholeness, putting things in proper perspective and preventing us from going into crisis mode. By taking deep breaths, I am able to connect to my core, becoming instantly more present and integrated. Charged breathing activates the fight-or-flight response in the body, relaxing the body while becoming more alert. Inhale deeply and sharply through the mouth all the way into the chest and then let the air fall out while allowing all the muscles to relax with it. On the inhale the air must be forced into the chest cavity and not the belly. If you are unsure, place both hands at the pressure points under each collerbone to make sure it rises and falls. On the exhale, don't push or force the air out. I do at least three rounds of ten. If I get dizzy or lightheaded, I look around the room and call out colors and objects aloud to ground myself in the room and in the present. For example, black chair, green pillow, red cup etc. I recognize I am here and now, not then and there, in my childhood trauma. I am grounded in my body. Colors and objects appear in sharp focus. I feel energy surging through my body. I'm aware of my own vitality and sexuality. While I'm fully charged, I try to remember a time in my early years when I felt the same wounding and mark the connection, recognizing this as an old injury. I ask the little girl inside what she needed to hear in that situation to make it all right and what she needs now in the current event to feel safe. Messages taken from the book, The Intimate Couple, "I love you, I want you, you are special to me, I see you and I hear you, you can trust your inner voice, it's not what you do, but who you are that I love, I'll take care of you"[2] are all helpful. The messages should match. The necessary childhood message should parallel the message needed in the current event.

As an adult, I have the power to give those messages to myself. When I'm less fragmented, I can receive and absorb the appropriate messages to feel safe again. I needed to hear that I was special as a child, and I need to hear that now. I can tell myself that I am important. I don't need my partner to show up to my book signing to confirm my value. The belief that I'm unimportant is an erroneous one created in my childhood; I have been carting it around for years unconsciously seeking out

2. Jack Lee Rosenberg, Beverly Kitaen-Morse, The Intimate Couple (Georgia: Turner), 27.

153

people and situations to confirm that belief. Every time I'm triggered by something, it's the same thought that is conjured up to hold me back from being my full, radiant self in my full power and exuberance.

I would often catch myself shallow breathing. I used to fear that if I took deep breaths I would be forced to confront my feelings. My diaphragm was shut down, and my pectoral muscles surrounding my heart were tight and rigid. I eventually got sick because holding stress in the body for prolonged periods of time wreaks havoc. Stagnation causes things to wither and die. Stagnant energy is a breeding ground for disease. When the body is in survival mode for extended periods of time, the adrenal glands have to work harder to produce the required hormones. Cortisol and norepinephrine, if secreted in the body in more than small spurts, create stress, weakening the immune system, leaving us susceptible to a myriad of illnesses.

As Transformational CPR began to take shape in my life, I was breathing deeply and seeing clearly. The new insights I was having were shifting my behavior and my focal point dramatically. Concern for my mental health was dominating my need to be right. My values were being reorganized in a healthy way. I was now able to give myself the validation I had been seeking since childhood. As long as I was in touch with my feelings and treated others with respect, being right or proving my point had little importance. My priority shifted to maintaining peace at all costs, and because of this shift in perception, I felt more peaceful most of the time.

When I released my judgments and opinions about others, I was naturally less attached to outcomes. I could allow others to be themselves and do what felt right to them. I didn't try so hard to control their behavior. I was able to release my resentments. No more playing the victim. I was free as long as I continued to choose mindfully.

Once my core beliefs changed so did my actions toward others. Making what I thought about myself more important than what others thought of me changed the way I behaved, allowing me to decide what to tolerate and what to eliminate from my life. Setting healthy boundaries in order to take care of myself became easier. Once my actions changed, naturally, the results in my life shifted.

I used to replay the memory of my hero brother pushing me into the pool repeatedly. I was still trying to understand why someone I loved so much would want to hurt me. I wasted hours trying to make sense of his actions. Perhaps the impact would be less painful if I'd had an explanation to justify his actions. I remembered how upset my mother was that afternoon he pushed me into the swimming pool. I grew angry thinking about all the injustices that were done to me over the years, making it difficult for me to trust people. I blamed my brother for my inability to find love in my life. When we feel persecuted, we perpetuate our suffering; when we wait for someone else to liberate us, we disempower ourselves completely.

The mind clutter of my past and the worries about my future made me angry and resentful, but I felt peace in the present moment. We use our stories as self-defining narratives to entrap us, delaying our happiness or making our well-being the responsibility of another person. Placing a higher value on tranquility over being right changed my state of mind radically. Forgiveness allowed me to find solace and reconnect with love, making happiness my responsibility.

I got anxious thinking about the future and the possibility of never surrendering my heart fully to another person. I decided that what had happened was in the past. By accepting things exactly as they were, I was able to move forward without any need to change them. It's impossible to forgive when we are holding tightly to the past. When we are invested in our story, we cannot forgive others or ourselves. Only in the present can we accept things. Blaming others keeps us bound and miserable. The realization that I had the power to change my thoughts was liberating. This meant that I could change the way I felt. When we take responsbility for our feelings, we recognize we are free.

PART THREE

Receptivity: The Third Step in CPR
(Awakening the Heart to Receive More Love)

Chapter 23
Moving On

I was beginning to understand things on a deeper level, but I didn't trust that I could handle obstacles every time they arose. I was still afraid of my emotions, especially grief, loss, and feelings of separation. Feeling good and meditating regularly are easy in the absence of a crisis, but when the shit hits the fan, it's easy to forget everything and revert back to negative thought patterns and unhealthy coping strategies.

I was in the final quarter of graduate school completing my master's degree in clinical psychology. Challenging my ego mind in order to experience more peace motivated me to contemplate a change in my career path. I felt compelled to continue with more self-introspection and, along with that, to help others do the same. It had been a long time since I was a student, but I had always had a fascination with psychology. I was tired of not having control over my career as an actress, always waiting and relying on others to dictate if and when I worked. I wanted a more satisfying career, one in which I could make a difference in people's lives, but the decision to study psychology did not sit well with my father. Nothing I chose was ever good enough. He never agreed with my choices in romantic partners, careers, or anything else. I realized that the disapproval gene had been a hand-me-down from his mother. I had come to expect his disapproval, but it still hurt me deeply.

Regardless, I made the commitment to enter into a psychology program. I was committed to following my intuition for guidance rather than allowing other people's judgments to sway my decisions. Ironically, I ended up at the same school that Dr. Nelson had attended years earlier. She and I discussed therapy as a profession when I was in treatment. The seed had been planted. I was excited about my new path in clinical psychology. I started writing at the same time. In graduate school, all we did was read and write papers, and I was inspired to explore writing in depth.

I had an idea for a screenplay. Over tea one day, I told my friend Tony of my radical thoughts on Western medicine and how I felt my mother was a prime example of how so many uninformed people get manipulated by the medical model and suffer through the consequences. He was excited about the political connotations of the subject matter and asked if he could help me write the screenplay.

We shared a passion to inform people and raise awareness on the corruption in health care and the influence of the pharmaceutical industry. The motivation for the unscrupulousness was completely monetary, and we were motivated to expose the erosion that had been taking place for far too long. I agreed to a partnership, thinking two minds must be more powerful than one. I thought it might help discipline me if I had someone to whom I held myself accountable.

We set a writing schedule for the next month. We met a few times a week, and our sessions were productive.

Since the story was based on true facts, we had plenty of reading material to keep us busy in between meetings. As time went on, however, our schedules changed, and arranging meetings became more arduous. I was feeling frustrated by the long pauses in between sessions. I was anxious to complete the project. I was finished with my graduate program and had time to devote to writing.

My best friend, Jenny, and I decided to take off for four days to get some rest and relaxation. We found some off-the-beaten-path hideaway in Mexico that was pristine but rustic. It was at least an hour boat ride from any city. The beach was quiet except for the gentle hum of generators, the only source of electricity, in the background. Narrow, cobblestone streets opened up onto a tiny village where children ran barefoot and the smell of freshly baked bread wafted through the morning air. It was charming, yet primitive. The quietude and peaceful environment provided us with the downtime we were seeking. It was a complete change from the city life to which we had grown accustomed. I started writing and couldn't stop. My creativity was fueled in this pristine atmosphere. By the end of four days, I had completed more writing than my partner and I had accomplished in a month.

Frustrated by the limitations of having a partner and coordinating schedules, I realized I needed to make some changes when I arrived home. It was time to take the project off on my own, but I didn't know how to break the news to Tony. I made the decision to sublet my house for two months, return to this magical hideaway in Mexico, and finish my screenplay.

When I did speak to my partner, I promised I would credit him completely for his writing and if it sold, I would be willing to split whatever money was offered evenly. In spite of my generous offer, he didn't take the news nearly as well as I had hoped. He was furious. I needed some time to think things over, and he definitely needed time to cool off.

When I checked the messages that had accumulated on my machine during my four days out of town, one message caught my attention because of its urgency. A well-known Hollywood producer had called. He had gotten my phone number from the director of the community mental health clinic where I had been treating patients for the past two years. He was looking for an actress who also had experience as a therapist. I don't suppose there are many of us out there, but he was casting a television show, and they had already cast two of the three therapists. When we spoke, he informed me they were in need of one more therapist, but so far had been unable to find the right person. He wondered if I would meet him for a cup of coffee to discuss the project. I told him I had just come back from a trip and could see him in a week. He insisted on meeting me within the next two days and assured me that it would only take a few moments of my time. I reluctantly agreed to meet him the following morning.

I drove into town to meet "Mr. Hollywood" at an outdoor café on Sunset Plaza the next morning. We began talking, but he quickly interrupted to say, "To cut through the bullshit, you are exactly what I have been searching for over the past several months." Now he had my attention, since Hollywood has built a reputation on false promises and ego enticement. This must be a joke, I thought to myself. This sort of thing doesn't just happen. Being cast in a television series is next to impossible and is, at the very least, supposed to be a struggle. I had put acting behind me when I first entered graduate school and felt good about that decision. Now this producer was going to screw it all up for me.

He pleaded with me to visit the film company down the street to meet the other producers. "It's right down the street," he urged. This was one of the biggest television companies at that time. I would have killed for an opportunity like this a few years ago. I had released my dream of being an actress, and here it was being served to me on a platter.

He waltzed me into the film company. Producers filtered into the large, glass-enclosed room with a stunning view of the Hollywood panorama portrayed in films. Nothing much happened in this brief encounter, but everyone was treating me like I was already a star. The buzz in the room was palpable. I was feeling good about myself and ready for anything. I was accustomed to walking into an audition and feeling like a piece of meat with hundreds of other beautiful girls sizing me up, trying to intimidate me, staring me up and down hoping for one thing, my failure. I was a bit suspicious of this treatment by the Hollywood bigwigs, who were swarming in and out of the room like bees to a honey pot.

After a handful of introductions to various producers and executives, "Mr. Hollywood" escorted me to my car, assuring me they loved me and promising to set up a screen test. A screen test means they are serious about hiring you but want to make sure you photograph well and the chemistry with the other actors' sizzles on film.

The date was set, and all I had to do was show up. The worst part about the whole thing was now I wanted it to happen and that made me nervous. I knew my ego was engaged, and that threw me off balance. The questions began swirling in my head. *What was I going to wear? How should I do my hair? What if I made a big mistake? What if they changed their minds?* All the old feelings from my acting days came rushing back. I felt special, important, like I was wanted, and yet I knew it was all an illusion. I felt like I was being tested one last time, but my attachment to booking the role at this point convinced me I was far too engaged.

For actors, there is so much emphasis on wanting to please others and worrying about what others think. When I was an actress, most of my time was spent outwardly focused and not inwardly focused in any way; I was always second-guessing what they wanted me to be. It was the opposite of everything I was learning from meditation, the Buddhist monk, yoga and diametrically opposed to the work I was doing as a clinician, but the opportunity seemed too big to pass up. I had to at least give it my best shot and see where it led.

Acting had caused me so much anxiety and turmoil for so many years. I had finally broken free of all that drama and chosen a different path that was more satisfying and nurturing to my psyche, but clearly, my ego was being tested.

Now that I had completed my studies and was seeing patients, my career looked promising. It was an exciting road ahead filled with a sense of purpose. I was passionate about my screenplay and had important things to share with the world. I was getting a lot of satisfaction guiding people out of their darkness and into the light as I continued doing my work.

Meeting the producer was a serious derailment from my recent decision to return to Mexico, finish my project, and decompress from society before starting my private practice. I was excited about my change in career, which felt divinely guided, but returning that one phone call had opened a huge doorway of doubt. Playing a lead character in an episodic television show would mean a big change in lifestyle. It was daunting, and I was confused.

I showed up for the screen test, gave my best audition, and was eventually told I had passed with flying colors. I couldn't quell my excitement. I was seeing dollar signs and all my student loans being paid off in one shot. I was being sucked in by the illusion that something outside of me was going to provide the missing pieces of my life, as though it would give me happiness and a sense of importance once and for all.

I started believing the offer was real just as everything fell apart. The network in New York requested I screen test a second time. They wanted to see me on film with the other two actors to make their final decision. In retrospect, I should have refused, but I didn't know I had the option. Agents typically advise their clients on such matters, but I had given up my agent and my manager long ago. It was laborious screen testing the first time, but now I had to show up and do it all over again. I was angry but couldn't say no, so I did a second screen test.

Next came the familiar game of waiting. In Hollywood, it's often referred to as "hurry up and wait". Waiting by the phone made me feel like such a loser. During this delay, I had several conversations with my writing partner, which didn't help me feel better. I guess the cooling off period only heated things up for him. He was livid and felt slighted. I didn't know how to make him still feel a part of the project and do what felt right in my heart.

The next day, I got a call from the producer informing me the show was being cancelled. Just like that and there was no discussing it. When Hollywood needs you, it's imminent, but when they don't need you, you're dropped with no explanation. I don't know what happened, but suddenly the deal was yanked away from me before I had any time to even decide if it was something I really wanted. Everything had suddenly gone from light to dark in a matter of days.

Smash cut to Tony threatening me with formulating a similar story with no credit to me. Everything had been going so well, and in a matter of days, my whole life was turned upside down, spinning me into feelings of worthlessness. All the old beliefs came flooding back.

Within a week, I was on my back with pneumonia again, so sick I couldn't get out of bed. It felt like my chest was being compressed, and I could hardly breathe. I was unable to read or watch movies this time. All I could do was think about my life and cry. I had never sobbed so hard in my life, crying for days on end. This was clearly the time to unleash all the grief and sorrow I had stored up over the years. I've heard pneumonia referred to as the grieving disease, and that truth was being revealed to me now. In Chinese medicine, the lungs are associated with grief. I felt like I was drowning in my own sorrow, and if I didn't start emptying my lungs immediately, I knew I would drown.

Chapter 24
Dark Night of the Soul

The second round of pneumonia was the catalyst for major changes. It's hard to find the blessing when chest deep in crisis and drowning, but as long as I was on my knees, I figured I might as well talk to God. I will refer to this one night as my "dark night of the soul." I am sure that phrase has many different connotations depending on whom you ask, but my version goes something like this. I'm sicker than a dog. My fever is at an all-time high. I'm in my tiny apartment, feeling horrible and exhausted, no matter how much sleep I've had. The amount of sleep I'm getting while harboring this illness appears to be completely inconsequential. I am utterly depleted.

It doesn't help matters that every time I feel the slightest bit of energy, I get up and start to do things around the house. Before long, I realize how tired I am and have to lie down again. At some point during the evening, I start to feel better (again) and get out of bed to watch a movie, the big event for the week. Halfway through the movie, I start feeling lousy. My fever burns with such intensity I fear my blanket will catch fire. I can feel the life force being drained out of me and try to lie down, but it only makes matters worse. I have difficulty breathing. It feels as though an elephant is sitting on my chest.

It gets worse as the clock ticks on. The walls are caving in, and the lights are fading. I'm scared. I'm sure this is what it must feel like moments before death. I start flashing on past memories; sure this is the final hour. *What to do? Do I call someone? Should I phone 911?* I want to, except I can't muster the energy to get up and make my way over to the telephone across the room. Here it is the end of my life, and I can't even say my good-byes. *What will people think? Will they assume it was a suicide? An overdose?* In a series of flashbacks, I can see and feel the critical events of my life one at a time.

I remember reading about this once. I am finally able to feel the emotion behind each crisis that I hadn't allowed myself to feel at the time. Surrender is the only option because of sheer exhaustion. I can't fight any longer.

I flash back on the abortions I had neatly tucked away with so many other events from my past. I feel the sadness and the loss of those unborn children. After dropping into the grief fully, I'm able to apologize to the unborn infants. More important, I'm able to forgive myself and release it once and for all. I flash on all the failed relationships from my past and all the hurtful things that transpired with previous partners. After allowing myself to chomp on the bitterness, digest the sweetness, and release the sorrow, I'm able to forgive them all, including myself. I flash on my father, who never was good at showing up for important events in my life or supporting my decisions. He was doing the best he could, and I knew that now. I knew there was more to process, but I'm unafraid this time. I invite the feelings so I can give them the acknowledgment they deserve instead of turning my back. By doing this, I'm able to experience the feelings and gently allow my heart to envelop the sadness, shame, and anger in pure love and acceptance. I'm not going to abandon myself any longer.

I give myself over fully to the process that had begun. Overcome with gratitude for all the people and circumstances in my life, I realize that each and every event of my past has made me the person I am today. My fever begins to subside. The walls in the apartment retreat and the lights grow brighter. My heart is open and alive with radiant light.

I was performing Transformational CPR on myself. It's not just a concept or an understanding; I am living it, breathing it, experiencing it completely. As my heart opens, I regain consciousness. I can breathe again. I'm willing to be totally present with whatever comes up without any judgment or need for things to be different than they are. Even if death is imminent at this moment, I am willing to accept that too. I am moved into total receptivity as I surrender the need to control any of it. This state of receptivity is allowing me to receive loving thoughts about myself, and for that, I am grateful. I am giving myself the gift of love. I know an emotional relapse is inevitable, but having direct experience of total freedom, even if only for one moment, leaves an impression. I'm allowing myself full access to the love inside my own heart. I yell, "I love you!" out loud. "I am here for you now and always." It feels so good to shout those words out and accept them as the truth. I am embodying all that I had been learning. Allowing my heart to break completely is giving me direct experience of absolute freedom and total love. No more bondage. The body never lies, and my body is responding positively.

Chapter 25
Heart Cracked Open

I was committed to meditating every morning and every evening for twenty minutes. At first, it was mostly twenty minutes of noticing how active my mind was, but that did not deter me. Twenty minutes seemed like an eternity, but it became easier with time and I noticed some shifts in my awareness. I could choose the thoughts on which to focus, and I could choose which to ignore. The only way negative thoughts could have power over me was if I gave them my attention. I was no longer denying thoughts and feelings as they arose; it didn't serve me in the past, and it wasn't serving me now.

When a negative thought emerged, I acknowledged it and then released it without a running commentary. I resisted the temptation to judge whether it was a "good" or a "bad" thought and simply brought my attention back to my mantra. When I allowed disturbing thoughts to fester, they would inevitably provoke negative feelings, taking me on a tangent and distracting me from my peaceful meditation.

Once I was more successful in meditation, I practiced the same principles in the world while going about my daily tasks. This process started to have a profound effect on my life and on all those with whom I came in contact. In the same way I learned to train my body physically, I could train my mind. Focusing on the present and not allowing negative thoughts about the past or future to distract me was the doorway to my core self where peace resides.

I continued attending weekly meditation meetings with the Buddhists in the canyon, which was helping my individual practice. It was comforting to have a support system I could rely on at any time. I found that meditating in a group was powerful and kept me plugged into a community that was as committed to self-improvement as I was.

I jumped back into my yoga practice with greater dedication and commitment. I found a teacher with whom I resonated and practiced four to five days a week. A sense of calm replaced my anxiety. My teacher had a knack for finding an individual's challenged area, and he gently invited him or her to explore deeper. He focused on one thing with me specifically, and that was opening my heart. While lying on our backs, in the final pose, "Savasana," in which we emulate a corpse, we can integrate all that we practiced in the ninety-minute class. The yoga master put a block under my heart and between my shoulder blades, which encouraged my shoulders and my pectoral muscles to let go. He placed a second block on the back of my head to support my neck. He had me hold this opening heart posture every time we did Savasana (resting pose) for the next several months.

One morning, as I lay on blocks with my shoulders back and my chest open, tears gently rolled down the sides of my face; I had no idea what they were about, but it felt good to let go, allowing my heart to burst open. After class, the teacher came over and held me for a long time. My heart melted, and I did nothing to stop it. I felt no judgment, just love and support from him, which was a totally new experience for me. I was accustomed to being teased or shamed by my brothers or father for being vulnerable.

Yoga helped me explore the deeper recesses of my psyche. It brought my awareness to areas I had shut down, especially my heart. My body posture reflected what was going on internally—my shoulders were rounded, my pectoral muscles were tight, and my diaphragm was restricted. As I began to loosen the muscles around my chest, my heart opened. I began to trust people more. As I began trusting more, I began to attract more trustworthy people.

One night, at our weekly meeting, the Buddhist master was discussing the nature of suffering. After a blissful pause, he stated, "You already are perfect peace and total joy at the center of your being. If you are feeling anything other than peace or joy, you have lost the ability to align with your true nature. In essence, you have lost your ability to reconnect with your inner child. You have become too serious and self-important, allowing your ego to dictate your every move, creating an existence prone to suffering."

I reflected over the course of my life, recalling all the resentments and hurts I had coveted. I thought about

Jonas's dishonesty with me over the years. I considered Brian and his outbursts of jealousy, how victimized I had felt, and the bitterness I'd felt toward Alex for lying to me about his girlfriend. I thought about my father and his inability to show up for me at important junctures and my mother, who couldn't tolerate my feelings. I remembered all the disappointments with acting jobs gone south. The anger I refused to let go of was my unwillingness to experience love. The lack of forgiveness was causing me extraordinary pain and suffering. I flashed all the way back to my near-drowning incident at the age of three. The flashback came like a flood of white light. It wasn't until now that I was able to see the connection between the act of CPR that my mother had performed on me and Transformational CPR (what I had begun practicing), which involves great self-awareness, self-acceptance, and forgiveness. It encompassed letting go of resistance, opening our hearts, and receiving and giving love freely.

Cardiopulmonary resuscitation is the attempt to take someone who is unconscious and bring him or her back to a state of consciousness by rejuvenating the heart organ. Transformational CPR returns us to our natural state of being by reviving the spiritual heart and requires awakening oneself to a more conscious state. When we release resentments and judgments, allowing our hearts to open fully, we can experience the love at the core of our being. In the wake of forgiveness, there is only peace.

In the same way we can revive and awaken the unconscious body with CPR, we can activate the spiritual heart, thus gaining access to true, everlasting peace, joy, and love.

Love is all I had ever longed for throughout my life. I didn't want to feel separation; I wanted to feel connection. I wanted to wake up! I wanted to expand my awareness so I could live a happy and deeply fulfilling life, which is my birthright, as it is yours. Pain is a great motivator and was the initial reason I was determined to wake up and put an end to the misery that I knew was self-imposed. I desperately wanted to experience what the monk kept insisting was beneath my thoughts and my body, at the center of my being. My beliefs and emotions stand alone as do the events and circumstances of my life, but they are not the truth of who I am. The core self is eternal. Everything else is temporary, and yet I spent so much of my life trying desperately to get love from things that were temporary and constantly changing.

My clarity revealed how the opinions I held about others created my suffering. My attachment to how things "should be" created the doubt, worry, and fear that I experienced so frequently. My thoughts kept me from being present. If I entered into a situation with an expectation, I was setting myself up to be disappointed. There is a clear distinction between pain and suffering. Pain is a part of the human condition; while suffering is an unnecessary experience we create by giving our thoughts and beliefs such power and validity. By allowing the succession of thoughts, past or future, we resist the present and succumb to the meanderings of the mind.

I wanted to know what was beyond my mind, beyond my crazy thoughts. What was beneath my anger, resentment, and fear? The witnessing part of me, the part that does not identify with these negative thought forms and limiting beliefs, is who I truly am. Who I am is reflected in the silence. Who I am is free from judgments and negative thought forms. Who I am is love and peace.

Most of the negative core beliefs I held, I later discovered, were a direct result of my early conditioning and had no validity whatsoever. I wanted to be free of all of the beliefs and judgments that were so clearly affecting my life and dictating my mood at any given time. I longed to keep this awareness in the forefront at all times. I was ready for new programming that would serve me instead of sabotaging my desires.

While dancing, I used to imagine what it might feel like to run my life with my heart and not my head—the way I did while dancing. I imagined how blissful it would be to enter into situations without protecting my heart. I wondered how it would feel to not allow fear to stand in my way and how liberating it would be to surrender to the flow of life and release resistance once and for all. As I looked around the room, I imagined most of these people starving for that same miracle in their lives. Consciousness is our natural state, but if we don't get quiet and go inside, we lose access to the still, small voice.

The monk was proposing that through self-investigation, we would come to discover that we already are happy, fulfilled, and at total peace at the core of our being in every instance. The irony is that we're all searching so desperately that we don't recognize what we already have. "Does that mean, when I come from a place of lack and limitation, that will become my experience?" I asked him. "Of course," he answered with a knowing grin.

If we believe we are lacking love, we will continue to perceive people and circumstances that replicate the absence of love. I had attracted many people into my life who had affirmed my unworthiness. I had been choosing people and situations that constantly disappointed me because I expected them to let me down. I realized that my distrust of others was a reflection of the lack of trust in myself. I would continue to experience betrayal until I released those negative beliefs. It was time to break the cycle.

Chapter 26
Eyes Wide Open

I was reviewing my own life over the past several years. I knew what it felt like to search desperately and how each new purchase or change I would make brought about the slightest bit of hope that "this" might finally fill the emptiness. There was always the possibility that the next relationship would save me. I clung to each partner, one after the other, for my salvation. But nothing ever seemed to fill the despair I felt inside. Some turn to religion, relationships, money, or fame, which on their own are not problematic. It's the hope that these things will save us that sets us up for the inevitable disappointment and the ultimate disillusionment. Hope keeps us living in the future and prevents any possibility of being present. It's like a dangling carrot that is always just out of reach. No matter how close we get, it will always be unattainable because fulfillment is not on the outside. True fulfillment can only be found once we stop reaching, searching, and hoping.

Everything external is a temporary Band-Aid. Everything changes, ends, or dies, and our searching begins anew. The answer is not out there. I am responsible for my happiness. Love had been inside, at the core of my being, waiting patiently to be discovered all this time. And all the while, I had been frenetically avoiding going inside and being with myself. I had been avoiding the silent monster. I was afraid to turn on the light and meet my monster. "If you don't go within, you will certainly go without," one of my teachers used to say. Until I was willing to do so, peace would remain illusory.

Going inside is the only real escape from pain and suffering. The irony is that I had been trying to dodge my pain and suffering by avoiding stillness, denying my feelings, and praying that the feelings would subside. Fulfillment is an inside job. Sometimes, it is difficult to see what is right in front of us. The sun shines every day. There are many days when we cannot see the sun because of the cloud cover, but it's always present. Just because we can't see or feel it, does not mean it isn't there. Faith is all we have on cloudy days.

I remember hearing a parable once about two fish swimming together upstream, trying to make it to their destination before spawning season was over. They had been swimming for days. Finally, the baby fish turned toward its mother and said, "Mommy, Mommy, I am really thirsty." The mother looked over at her son and giggled. "Honey, don't be silly, you are surrounded by water. All you have to do is open up and let it in." Disregarding the value of what we have in front of us makes things more difficult than they need to be. We tend to dismiss the things that appear simple, as if simple is not worthy, as if struggle builds character and adds value.

By searching for love and peace outside of ourselves, we distract ourselves from our natural state. I see the chasing of material goods coupled with the belief that these will create happiness and fulfillment as sheer avoidance. It keeps us from being fully present; we hang on to the hope that salvation is around every corner. *As soon as I book the lead in the next big feature, then I will be happy. I will feel secure when I buy that Porsche I have been admiring. I will experience peace as soon as I find my soul mate.* Do any of these statements sound familiar? Of course they do, because we have all been trained to think that fulfillment is outside of us. This would be an appropriate time to perform Transformational CPR on oneself. In this state, we are identified with the ego mind and not the authentic self. The ego keeps us in a state of wanting but never satisfied. If we are projecting into the future by thinking how happy we will be sometime down the line, we cannot possibly be present to what is happening now. Likewise, pining away over past events or feeling remorseful or guilty about something that has already happened is a distraction from being present to the moment.

My own unconsciousness and refusal to look inside and get quiet was a clear resistance. What lay underneath that resistance was fear, which kept me from experiencing peace. My attachment to my conditioning led to my victimhood. Limiting thoughts and judgments kept me from being present with the love inside and kept me from experiencing true, everlasting peace. I had been a hostage to my mind.

Chapter 27
Scar Tissue

Children trust effortlessly and automatically. Most youngsters are completely surrendered and rest in a space of receptivity. Perhaps being dependent on their elders for survival keeps them in a place of receptivity. It's not until negatively perceived things happen that we slowly shut down our hearts. Numerous things can instill fear and cause us to contract our bodies both physically and emotionally. Over time, we are offered food that is sour or rotten, and it makes our body sick. We are met with challenges that weaken our immune system. We fall down and break a bone or sprain tendons and ligaments.

We begin to comprehend that our body ages over time and is susceptible to illness, disease, degeneration, and eventually death.

What hurts even more is the realization that our hearts can be broken. People disappoint us and people leave; our feelings get hurt, which can often move us into a fearful, closed-off state. When I hold onto old beliefs, it affects my behavior in the present. My father's disapproval of my choices and his inability to show up for pivotal moments in my life led me to believe that I wasn't good enough. An underlying, unconscious belief that I was not good enough affected my actions and choices for many years. When I reached any level of success, I found ways to sabotage myself. Other negative beliefs, such as, love hurts and I will be disappointed, forced me to push people I cared about away for fear they would hurt me, making it difficult to have an intimate relationship. How many of us carry that story and aren't aware of it?

We erect walls to protect ourselves from being heartbroken, which keeps people out, but also keeps us frozen in isolation. I realized how lonely I was when my heart was shut down and I couldn't allow others to get close. Paradoxically, I thought I was protecting myself from potential heartache, when in fact, I was actually causing more suffering by avoiding connection and intimacy with others.

Before the age of three, I trusted my older brother Rick so implicitly. I never dreamed that he would do anything to hurt me or put me in danger. I didn't have a precon- ceived idea of what pain was yet. I had no paradigm for sorrow or separation. Life was perfect, safe, and friend- ly. That first realization that life wasn't completely safe, due to my near-death experience at the early age of three and the feeling of being betrayed by my beloved brother etched a deep scar. My innocence had been lost. No longer would I perceive things realistically, instead I would look through a filter of deception. Without any awareness, I would continue to find evidence of a precarious world and the need to keep my heart protected. I had been dragging around the belief that the world was perilous, so the world became somewhat treacherous for me.

The body wants to heal. When we cut ourselves, the body goes to work repairing itself. First, we grow a scab to pro- tect the raw and broken skin, and when it is time, the scab falls off leaving unbroken, renewed skin. The same thing happens on an emotional level. There is a desire, a hunger even, in most of us to return to our natural state of wholeness. When we do connect to that place, it feels like going home and we're certain it's right. I was still struggling to get back to that childlike state of open receptivity and trust. I had new awareness's and had experienced my core, but I wasn't convinced that I could maintain direct experience of my authentic self. Where did the innocence go? I wondered. I eventually got to a place where I would welcome a challenge as another opportunity to gain presence and wake up in consciousness. I was diligently practicing Transformational CPR. I was learning to activate my heart and open myself to love rather than close down and remain encased in fear. I decided to choose love by forgiving all the negative thoughts as they arose.

Carl Jung, the world-renowned psychoanalyst, believed that humans have an innate drive to self-actualize. Jung was influential throughout my studies in psychology and spirituality. He talked about man's search for his own spiritual enlightenment and devoted his entire life to studying matters of higher consciousness. Socrates, one of the great philosophers of our time, once said, "An unexamined life is a life not worth living."

For many years, I wanted to regain that innocence and trust I felt as a child because I knew that was total freedom. I wanted to release painful thoughts of separation and welcome my feelings, but fear still held me captive at times. I was a victim and would remain disempowered until I was willing to face the truth fully and completely without any hiding, but I was still compelled to remain unattached in case someone hurt me. These stubborn thoughts would plague me and keep me up at night. I struggled with the internal conflict of craving intimacy and connection and the terror of being hurt and disappointed. The only thing that worked was noticing the thoughts that I knew were illusions and without judgment simply guiding my attention to connect to a deeper truth I knew existed.

Our primary caregivers may not be in tune with our needs, so we grow up thinking we are deficient in some way. We grow up trying to fill the emptiness instead of allowing the emptiness to fill us. We attempt to fulfill our unmet needs from childhood by projecting those needs onto our intimate partners. When we do not get what we want, we become disappointed and blame others for that lack. This inevitably seems to catapult us right into the agonizing mind; thereby recapitulating the lie we learned in childhood that we are not good enough. Every time we reenact this old story, we carve a deeper groove in our brain, forcing the habit to enlarge, but each time we are able to catch ourselves and replace the lie with the truth that we are whole, we dig another groove that eventually becomes more dominant through repetition.

The heart wants to heal just the same as the physical body, so by attracting things that trigger our wounds, it gives us an opportunity to experience our feelings and heal the traumas of our past. If we avoid feelings, they come back stronger. This stuff isn't so difficult. Most of us make it harder than it has to be.

Chapter 28
Vast as the Ocean

I was invited to a silent meditation retreat. I'd been on many yoga retreats, but none where silence was a requirement. I was now convinced that pushing myself beyond my comfort zone leads to deeper wisdom and more self-awareness. The more I held on to comfort and resisted pain, the more suffering I encountered. When I was able to let go, things seemed to flow more gracefully and less painfully.

Knowing we would be in silence for eight days brought up all my fears. *What if I can't be quiet for that long?*

What if I can't sit still in meditation? Will my thoughts haunt me? Will I want to leave early? I thought about backing out several times. I had visions of various escape plans dancing in my head. I imagined feigning illness and running out with my hand covering my mouth to prevent vomiting or simulating an emergency call from home requiring my immediate return. Numerous colorful scenarios passed through my mind as Friday approached. I stood by and watched them all pass through my head while guiding my attention back to the present without judgment. Now that I had a considerable private practice, I knew I had a responsibility to my clients, as well as myself, to process my feelings and face the challenges that arose.

The following Friday, I bid my cats farewell and hit the road. It was a slow drive along the coast heading north. The further north I went, the more wild crashing waves on rocky, jagged cliffs became the landscape I was privy to. I was still a little apprehensive about the next few days, but the beauty on the drive was calming my spirits, keeping me incredibly present.

I can remember the long drive into the retreat center at Zaca Lake, the year before. I had to drive carefully the closer I got to the entrance of the retreat center to avoid hitting the numerous deer that crossed the road. Once inside the gate, the camp host at Zaca, an elderly man, greeted me. His sweet smile revealed a mouthful of missing teeth. He gave me my room key and a map of the grounds. There were numerous little cottages nestled around a taintless lake. Gentle rolling hills surrounded the property as well as countless oak trees that looked as though they had been there since the beginning of time. I was told that this sacred land belonged to the Chumash Indians.

Esalen, located in Big Sur, the location of the current retreat, boasts natural hot springs that sit out on the cliffs overlooking the magnificent Northern California coastline. I was given my room key and had time to unpack and soak in the tubs before check-in. The hot sulfur pools melted away my fears, prompting the detoxification process to begin. Once I checked in, I knew silence would commence.

The entire experience from start to finish was magical. Oddly, the silence was the easiest part. There was no need to speak. We had several sittings of guided mediation. I made it a point to attend the optional kirtan every morning and evening. Kirtan is devotional East Indian music that is more like chanting than singing. It's typically led by one or more musicians in a call-and-response style and is designed to call on the presence of the divine. The musicians sing a verse, and then the audience echoes it. Typically, there is a tabla player (Indian percussions), someone on harmonium, and some on bells and other percussion-like instruments. Kirtan is uplifting and inspirational music that opens the heart. Chanting the same verses repeatedly, I fell into a trance-like state totally focused on Spirit. We continued to chant the names of different Hindu deities until my entire body and mind dissolved. I was one with all existence. I had surrendered into a deep and blissful state.

The only thing that could pull me away from this ecstatic chanting was mealtime. Each meal was intentionally prepared for us with love and blessings. Most of the food was organically grown on the property in the community garden. Everything was made fresh for each meal.

On the fourth day, I booked a massage on the deck of my room overlooking the ocean. I was getting closer to heaven, feeling better every day and sinking deeper into myself. I used to run from spending time with myself, but now I relished in it. I was accustomed to being the social butterfly, but in the silence, I was forced to give up making friends with everyone and extending my energy outward. This was a rare opportunity to delve inside and court myself, and I was taking full advantage.

The final day of the retreat fell on New Year's Day. On this sunny afternoon, the entire group walked in silence to the bluffs at the edge of paradise. We joined together at the top of the hill and formed a circle. Holding hands, we said a group prayer, and I felt the oneness that pervaded everything in that moment. *How was it that I used to convince myself that I was separate from divine love?* I absorbed the panoramic view from the top of the overhang as the circle broke up.

I was awestruck by the vastness of the ocean shimmering before me. Breathing in the freshness and feeling the breeze against my cheeks, I merged with the uncontainable infinity before me. With my heart expanded to maximum capacity, I made the connection between eternal spirit and the endless ocean before me. Spirit has no end and no beginning. It's infinite, whereas everything else in life is finite. When we tap into our source, we tap into the inexhaustible supply. There is no lack or limitation. There is only space and endless possibilities.

That afternoon was so striking and profound that I carry the image of the vast and boundless ocean view on those bluffs clearly in my mind as though it were yesterday. Anytime I start to feel small or feel I am losing my sense of connection to all that is, the image of that open space and endless horizon comes rushing back to remind me of the illusion that we are separate and that we are our thoughts and beliefs, the illusion that I have no control over how I feel or what thoughts I focus on, the illusion that we are separate from spirit, from God, from love, from everything.

One of the main difficulties I struggled with was staying present at all times. I let the childhood stories creep in and dictate how I felt. Old negative beliefs would filter in periodically, and if I weren't mindful, I would carelessly accept the provocative invitation to go down dark and dangerous mental alleys. Those familiar stories would fight for my attention, stories of not being good enough or not deserving total happiness and freedom, the constant worry about how things would turn out. I had to be diligent with my CPR, keeping myself plugged into the light.

The opportunity to be silent and watch my mind from a witnessing place without commentary was helpfull. I wanted to be able to bring all I learned on this retreat back to my everyday life. I'd had the opportunity to experience the truth of who I really am at my core for an extended period of time. At my core, I'm whole, complete, and perfect, as we all are. Staying connected to myself meant being courageous enough to stand in my truth at all times. Being truthful requires not abandoning myself. When I allowed myself to be manipulated by fear, I was unable to speak my truth, concerned that I might alienate another person. Shifting my intention to honor myself first sometimes meant being willing to lose someone I loved. Training the mind in this way helped to reorganize my values, making my authenticity the priority. If I continued meditating on a regular basis, I would have a chance of staying out of the madness of my mind. I have no business there, no matter how tempting it is. What other people think of me is none of my business. My only purpose is to stand in truth.

Getting quiet for eight full days and diving into deep self-investigation revealed some important axioms. Some of the insights I gained are: I know I can guide my thoughts if I am mindful. I can stop the train of never-ending negative beliefs by placing my awareness back on the present moment. Doubt, worry, and fear do not exist in the present moment; those are futuristic thoughts or past memories. Darkness cannot exist in light, and light is in the present. When I am present, I am in touch with my core, and that is a place of unconditional love. Separation only exists in the mind. I can allow thoughts to enter and watch the thoughts go by. If I don't attach to the beliefs or stories that follow, I remain committed to the truth and I remain present—just like in a meditation practice where I allow a thought to bubble up and without judgment or condemnation allow it to pass and return to my mantra.

I felt the invitation to stop, in this moment, at this time, and tell the truth. No more derailments. Getting honest means acknowledging the truth of whom I am. I am not my beliefs, I am not my thoughts, and I am not my body. I am willing to look inside and bring my attention back to the truth of who I am when I notice I'm caught in a story. It's the identification with negative stories that create my discomfort. If I drop the story, the suffering goes away. If I am still suffering, I know that I am still holding onto some part of a story. If I investigate further, I usually find that I still have thoughts or opinions robbing my attention. I must remain diligent. *I have to be willing to release the story, and the suffering will be transmuted,* I keep reminding myself whenever I feel my mind slip into its old habits. Henry David Thoreau said, "God himself culminates in the present moment, and will never be more divine in the lapse of all ages." Suffering cannot exist in the present, just as darkness cannot survive in the light.

Retreats are an opportunity to withdraw from the world temporarily to reflect and go inward. It's a chance to create a love affair with the self. Imagine entering into a relationship where you and your partner are connected to the pure love inside yourselves. The purity of two whole individuals joining together out of desire instead of need is the ultimate. I usually gain tremendous insight on retreats, which I bring back with me and integrate into my daily life. More important, retreats can offer an opportunity to sink deeper into the self, which ultimately connects us more deeply with everything and everyone around us. I can bring all of me wherever I go and to whomever I meet. I will not abandon myself when I most need my own support any longer.

Chapter 29
R for Receptivity
(The Third and Final Step)

Once I realized there was a systematic approach to manifesting peace and well-being, I grew very excited. The name Transformational CPR felt appropriate since this process did revive my heart and allow me access to the most expansive love imaginable. My near-drowning incident at such an early age left me gasping for air, but without the jump-start to reactivate my heart, I wouldn't be breathing. Without that activation, I would not be here today to tell this story. Transformational CPR is a simple, step-by-step process that brings us back to our true nature, allowing us to breathe deeply and comfortably, but most of all, it opens our heart and invites us to take part in the most profound love imaginable.

With Transformational CPR becoming a way of life for me, the anxiety I had grown accustomed to had vanished. I no longer felt guarded and protected, which invited deeper intimacy, and the relationships in my life radically improved. I had full access to the deeply rooted vitality in my body, and I felt a peace I never knew existed. I felt free.

Witnessing breakthroughs from those I worked with was confirmation that this system was effective for others as well, when put into action. I watched those I counseled taking responsibility instead of blaming others for their misfortune and unhappiness, empowering themselves by stepping out of victimhood, manifesting their desires, releasing guilt, embracing forgiveness, and busting through resistance. I saw their depression and anxiety dissipate. Harboring resentments of any kind keeps us from our joy.

I deemed the R, the third letter, in CPR as receptivity. When I dropped all the stories and got present, I noticed

I organically moved into a receptive state. Even though I've separated the three steps in Transformational CPR to write about them, the truth is each one bleeds into the next. They overlap and are intertwined. Each step takes it's turn, but none can be neglected if we want total happiness. Receptivity is being fully surrendered. It's similar to a childlike state of openness and trust, not just in mind but also in body. In trust mode, the body relaxes and opens. When we trust, our minds open to discover the truth of who we are, no matter what we are thinking. We move from contraction to openness.

Being willing to release my attachment to preconceived ideas made me a receptacle for innocence and divine creativity. I stopped blocking the flow of life. In this space of receptivity, divine guidance can dictate our every move and our lives take on a grace that is enormously powerful. True wisdom can come to us here. In this place, I could feed myself the spiritual nourishment I had been craving. I could fill myself up with any affirmation I felt appropriate at this time and actually take it in, believe it, and reap the full benefits. When we are in an open and receptive mode, it's the most optimal time to shift our thinking from erroneous self-destructive thoughts to positive thoughts that reflect our true nature.

In receptivity, we can experience gratitude for all the things and people in our lives. The more gratitude I experienced in my heart, the more I manifested things that made me grateful.

While receptive, I could feel my heart exploding. I felt full. Instead of the usual feelings of lack and limitation, I felt in touch with the infinite spirit. With my heart wide open, I felt the unfathomable creation of all things manifest and unmanifest. A sense of power and strength beyond all measure washed over me. The authentic self is the soul being revealed to us, and I was willing to completely embrace my full potential.

From this state of true receptivity, I understood, for the first time, what the quote from the Bible, "Seek ye first the kingdom of Heaven and all else shall be revealed unto thee," Matthew 6:33 (KJV) truly meant. The kingdom is inside of us. I always had the keys; I just hadn't realized it because I was too busy searching. Once we are at peace with ourselves, and no longer searching, we experience heaven, and heaven is on earth now.

If I could remain unattached to my stories and steer clear of the identification with my judgments, then I would have access to heaven, where all was possible. If I could raise my self-awareness by not giving negative thoughts any power, convinced the thoughts are false, and take steps to get myself present, I could move to the third step of receptivity successfully and effortlessly. Here, I was guaranteed to feel unconditional love, peace, and a sense of fulfillment. If I mastered these three steps successfully, then I could stop suffering. When this became apparent, I began to take this system that I call Transformational CPR seriously and felt inspired to share it with as many people as possible.

CONCLUDING THOUGHTS

Chapter 30
Passing the Torch

Through many years as a clinical psychotherapist, meditation teacher, and spiritual conselor, I have listened to and counseled hundreds of people facing life's challenges. Together, we have journeyed through change, expansion, and awakening. I have found that through consciousness, presence, and receptivity, anxiety and depression can be transformed into peace and contentment.

I continue teaching Transformational CPR today, helping people recognize their judgments and expectations and inviting them to examine how their thoughts keep them bound to unnecessary suffering. I facilitate workshops and offer relationship-coaching, assisting people in finding deep and fulfilling relationships with themselves as well as with others. I also speak publically to groups and organizations on leadership and empowerment. Ultimately, I empower others to become their own therapist.

Everyone wants to love and be loved. Through guidance and encouragement, I assist others in identifying whatever blocks them from connecting to their authentic self where true love resides. Taking responsibility for the part we play in a relationship instead of blaming others allows us to work more effortlessly and gain deeper self-awareness. Sometimes people forget that a relationship is an option, not a requirement. I continue guiding people to find love within themselves, whether they have a relationship or not, so they can function more magnetically in the world, attracting the right people.

If we call off the search for love in outside things—which we can do since love is available inside each of us all the time—we can stop demanding that our partners give us the love that we so desire. Once two people are connected to the eternal love inside of themselves, their union becomes stronger and their partnership becomes more about a desire rather than a clinging for survival or to a complacent comfort zone. When two people meet in their individual connections to inner strength, they experience a profound union. From here, real intimacy is possible. Because of Transformational CPR, I was finally able to stop self-abandoning and start trusting and honoring myself. I was capable of finding love in a deeply fulfilling relationship, but most of all, I was able to experience deep peace in a way that used to feel unattainable.

The human spirit continues to inspire and amaze me. I get the opportunity to witness my growth daily along with many others who continue to release anger and resentments they have harbored for years. The freedom we experience from the release that forgiveness provides is immeasurable.

I continue taking responsibility for my actions and my beliefs, while guiding others to do the same, thereby choosing empowerment over victimhood. We replace anger and resentment with gratitude and forgiveness, which provides the opening to liberation and empow- erment. Guiding others through breathing techniques while moving stagnation and trauma through the body removes the barriers to the authentic self and ends the cycle of ruminations and future projections. Being of service to others daily assists me in my constant evolution, as I watch my stories and expectations filter in and out. By neither identifying with the thoughts nor sublimating them, I remain present and convicted to the truth of who I am rather than my old negative beliefs about who I am.

I'm committed to this work because I benefit daily from it. I witness people riddled with anxiety move into a calm, peaceful existence. I thought I was doomed to fear and anxiety, but doing this work has led me to gratitude for the peace I have created in my life. The inspiration I feel daily from witnessing the constant awakening in my own spirit as well as in the spirits of those around me is what inspired this book. I wanted to share these steps with those of you who find yourself in a perpetual state of suffering as I did and with those of you who have not yet found your inner gift.

I feel blessed for all that I have learned and continue to learn and the ability to help others find the hidden gift inside of themselves. Once we discover that what we have been searching for our whole lives is already inside of us and has been there all along, our heart opens to all things possible. It frees us from the desperate need to rely on anyone or anything else to give us love.

Having a deep and profound love connection with another person is one of the most special things we get to experience in form, but with the realization that we no longer have to wait for someone else to give us love and validation comes liberation. When we let go of our expectations that another person should fix us or make us feel better about ourselves, we release disappointment and longing. When we own our thoughts, feelings, and actions, we can reclaim our power.

Having been born in the month of July makes me a Cancer. I once heard a friend say, "A Cancer would rather lose her entire claw than let go of someone." I used to feel that way, so it made me laugh, but when I examined the statement more closely, it made me sad. So much pain came from feeling hopelessly stuck in past relationships. Even when it was clear to me the relationship wasn't good for me, I still had trouble letting go because I fooled myself into thinking I needed someone else to validate my existence. I was willing to sacrifice my needs rather than trust in the miraculous. Leaving someone literally felt like losing a part of myself because I had so little access to my core self at the time. Losing my sense of self, when ending a relationship, was an illusion, but it took some time to learn how to get validation from within. Now, I have choices, and I am never stuck. I am free. I get to choose. I can breathe deeply. I show up for myself, and so can you, if you so choose.

Give yourself the gift of Transformational CPR. Learn to use your emotions as your barometer. If you are happy, then you are connected to your source. If you are unhappy, then you have allowed yourself to be derailed from your core; most likely, you are caught in a story of the past or the future but are certainly not present. Performing Transformational CPR is simply removing any blocks that keep you from experiencing your true nature.

I heard Marianne Williamson once say that when Michelangelo began creating his masterpieces, he didn't see before him just a slab of marble; he saw the perfect sculpture. It was his job to use his tools simply to chip away the excess, all that didn't belong, so the perfect sculpture could emerge. This is what we do with Transformational CPR. We chip away anything that is blocking our soul from emerging.

Don't be afraid to face your demons. Your fear of confronting those demons is the only thing that separates you from absolute freedom. The spiritual heart is closer than you imagine it to be. It's closer than the physical heart or the emotional heart. It's the heart at the core of your being. Any and all motion to find it implies a negation that it exists at the center of your being.

Accept the invitation to dive deep into yourself. I hope my sharing some of the lessons I have learned and continue to learn, will inspire you to grab the torch of enlightenment as you continue your journey through life. Ask yourself now if you are willing to let go of old negative beliefs that are keeping you stuck. It requires being totally honest and present as often as possible. Catch yourself falling into the old routine of blaming those around you when you don't get what you want. Be willing to let go of all the stories you carry and all the expectations you have of others. Allow your heart to open fully and forgive the people and circumstances of the past. Forgive yourself.

Notice a flower for the first time without your preconceived idea of what a flower should smell like or feel like. Let gratitude flood your heart and fill you.

Be willing to drop all stories of who you think you are and allow your true nature to be revealed. Open and receive the gift that is you. You are the present. You are the gift.